What some are saying…

"Your 'Bagel' book is what really got me fired up for my Jewish friends. It answered a long time yearning in my heart about how to talk about the Messiah in a personal way…"

–J. Proctor

"Thanks to Barry Rubin for his excellent book, You Bring the Bagels…"

–L. Campion

"I learned so much I never knew before. Now I can speak with confidence to both my Jewish and Christian friends…"

–A. Thompson

You Bring the BAGELS I'll Bring the GOSPEL

Other Books by Author

The Messianic Passover Haggadah
Lederer Books/Messianic Jewish Pub. © 1985, 2005 by Barry and Steffi Rubin

Dedicate & Celebrate: A Messianic Jewish Guide to Hanukkah
Lederer Books/Messianic Jewish Pub. © 1999 by Barry Rubin & Family

The Sabbath: Entering God's Rest
Lederer Books/Messianic Jewish Pub. © 1998 by Barry and Steffi Rubin

You Bring the BAGELS I'll Bring the GOSPEL

Sharing the Messiah with Your Jewish Neighbor

Barry Rubin

Lederer Books
a division of
MESSIANIC JEWISH PUBLISHERS
Clarksville, Maryland

Printed in the United States of America

10 09 08 07 7 6 5 4
ISBN 10: 1-880226-65-0
ISBN 13: 978-1-880226-65-0

Lederer Books
a division of
Messianic Jewish Publishers
P.O. Box 615
Clarksville, MD 21029

Distributed by
Messianic Jewish Resources International
Order Line: (800) 410-7367
E-mail: lederer@messianicjewish.net
Website:www.messianicjewish.net

TABLE OF CONTENTS

SECTION II

Your Message: The "Jewish Gospel"...*61*

SECTION III

Your Audience: Your Jewish Neighbor...*103*

SECTION IV

The Feedback: Barriers to Belief...*145*

FOREWORD

Many are the books and booklets telling us why and how we ought to share the life-giving message of the Gospel with our Jewish friends. Once in a while a book comes from the presses by a person who really has something meaningful to say. This latest work is by my friend Barry Rubin, who, from his training as well as experience, has provided us with an excellent book.

Believers everywhere have an intellectual comprehension that the message of the New Covenant must be shared with people of all nations, including our Jewish friends. While there are excellent books on how to share God's message with people in general, God's people need to know how best to share the Gospel message of Yeshua with their Jewish friends.

Barry Rubin begins first to encourage Gentile believers to talk effectively about their faith with Jewish people. It was a Gentile believer who shared with Barry so that he became a believer. He tries to encourage the people in the churches to actually put into practice being a good witness to a Jewish neighbor.

Barry has had excellent training in communications. He can apply those principles in such a way that the average non-Jewish believer can learn and then set out to do the job God has them to do.

The reader will find material on learning about the background and beliefs that might be barriers to a witness. Barry also shows us how we can overcome these barriers to have the best possible opportunity to communicate with our friends.

Of the greatest interest is Barry's analysis of how the master soul-winner, Yeshua, touched the hearts of people. His analysis of how Yeshua related to the Samaritan woman (John 4) is excellent and should give the average believer some expertise in how to relate to the needs of Jewish friends, and people in general.

The value of the book is enhanced by the use of numerous models that very quickly enable the believer to grasp the material and sharpen his understanding of how best to share.

Upon reading the book, I had a special blessing. You will be encouraged as you let Barry Rubin speak to your heart and allow him to guide you to be a more effective communicator as you share the Gospel with Jewish people

Louis Goldberg, Th.D. ז"ל
Professor Emeritus of Theology and Jewish Studies
Moody Bible Institute
Chicago, Illinois

PREFACE
TO THE REVISED EDITION

It finally happened! Dunkin' Donuts is selling bagels. Being a bagel *maven* (connoisseur), I've been carefully watching how popular bagels have been getting since the first edition of this book in 1989. If you can't find a bagel shop in your community, you're sure to find Lender's bagels in the frozen food section of your food store. The fact is, bagels are everywhere. In fact, I just learned that bagel shops are the fourth most popular new business in the country, behind computer-type businesses and tattoo parlors.

I've been doing some unofficial surveying and have come up with a conclusion: although bagels began as a Jewish food, little by little people stopped associating them with Jews. They've become *goyische* (Gentile).

When I was young, besides plain bagels, maybe we'd have onion bagels, garlic bagels, sesame seed bagels, and poppy seed bagels. Not a whole lot more. But now, Oy vey!

Blueberry bagels, banana bagels, strawberry bagels, and even—hold on to your hat—chocolate chip bagels. What was once oh-so-Jewish, is now oh-so-Gentile. Bagels have been assimilated. This is not so different from what happened to the Gospel.

What began as a thoroughly Jewish movement within Judaism is now so far from its Jewish roots that the Messiah is looked upon as the Gentile god. Jews can't follow a Gentile god. The Torah records what happened to our ancestors when they played around with paganism. Oy!

But Yeshua—Jesus—is not a Gentile god. He is the Messiah of Israel and Savior of the world, who came first to his own people. In fact, his primary service was to bring the chosen people closer to the God of Abraham, Isaac, and Jacob. He was the ultimate prophet.

The fact that so many Gentiles joined in is great! God told the Jews to be a light to the Gentiles. But what's happened over the past 2,000 years is that the Good News message, once so Jewish, has come to look non-Jewish.

It's like bagels. The Jews brought bagels to the Gentiles, but now the Gentiles have taken over and nearly forgotten the source of this delicious, low-fat roll. That's not so bad with bagels, but it's disastrous when sharing the bread of life with Jewish people. The Church needs to put the Messiah back in his Jewish context.

Your reading of this book will help you get a better perspective on how to reach out to Jewish people with the Good News that Messiah has come to atone for sin. I hope you'll remember that the Good News message was brought to the world by Jews, spread by Jews, and has a Jew at its core.

Don't let happen to this message what has happened to bagels. Yes, the new bagel is tasty (although I myself have never eaten and probably will never eat a fruit bagel; remember I'm a *maven*), but it's not Jewish. Christianity is tasty, but it's lost its Jewish flavor. Restoring it will help Jewish people be more comfortable biting into Yeshua, the bagel of life, and will help Gentiles receive a great blessing. That's what this book is all about.

So . . . enjoy!

PREFACE
TO THE FIRST EDITION

A Message for Believers

You are about to read this book because you care about Jewish people. You have experienced new life in Messiah and you want to share this Good News with a Jewish person you know. Perhaps you have a friend, co-worker, or even a relative who is Jewish. You want to tell him or her the Gospel message—the best news you've ever heard, the news that God has provided atonement for sin. Perhaps you have known this person for years but have not been able to discuss the Messiah. This book was written to help you share the love of Yeshua with his own Jewish people.

I will be discussing the principles I have taught as both a college teacher of communications and the director of several missionary training programs. My testimony is woven throughout the book to illustrate many of the principles you will learn.

Keep in mind, however, that your responsibility is only to present the message of the Messiah as clearly as you possibly can, prayerfully and lovingly. It is not your responsibility to cause your Jewish friend to believe. That work is in the hands of God.

As you read through this book, you will see references to your "Jewish neighbor." This word *neighbor* is used in the same sense that Yeshua used it in the story of the Good Samaritan. It might mean the friend next door, a distant relative, someone you work with, or anyone you encounter with a need for the Messiah. I picture you sitting down with some bagels, a cup of coffee or tea, and the Bible. What I hear is a neighborly chat about the Gospel.

From time to time I will use what is called *Messianic* terminology—"Christian" concepts expressed in a Jewish way. After discussing the benefit of this terminology in your witness in Section II, chapter 7, I use it exclusively throughout the rest of the book. This is to encourage you to become familiar with it, and to incorporate these Messianic terms into your own speech. It will make your message more effective.

A Message for Jewish People

You may be wondering why a Jewish person like me would be interested in teaching non-Jewish people how to persuade you to believe in Messiah At best, you may think that this is a waste of time. At worst, you may consider me a traitor to our people. I have one thing to say to you—truth is truth.

If Jesus—*Yeshua*, in Hebrew— is the promised Messiah, then it would make sense that Jews should believe in what he says. If he is not, then not only am I wasting time, but it would follow that all Christians are practicing a false religion and should look elsewhere for truth. Yeshua claimed to be our long-awaited Messiah. Either he is or he isn't.

In this book, although it is written to help non-Jewish followers of his communicate his message more effectively to you, you may discover that Yeshua really is who he said he is—the Messiah. Why not prayerfully ask God to show you the truth?

Once, an agnostic friend and I were having a discussion. It took a while, but he finally admitted that God's existence had nothing whatsoever to do with his faith or lack of it. Either God exists or he doesn't. My friend's belief or disbelief had no effect upon the reality of God. Logic tells us that God exists (or doesn't exist) regardless of what we believe.

So it is with the question of Yeshua. Either he is the promised one, the Messiah of Israel and the Savior of the world, or he is not.

Our belief does not make him the Messiah (Christ, in Greek); our unbelief does not make him fiction. Truth is truth.

I believe that Yeshua is exactly who he said he is—the Messiah. I came to this conclusion in 1973 and the longer I study and ponder his claims, the more convinced I am of their truth.

To Jewish people who read this book, I ask you to try to understand that Christians who purchase this book do so out of sincere love. They want to administer the antidote to man's greatest ailment—sin. The cure is found in Yeshua.

ACKNOWLEDGMENTS

A number of people contributed to this book, indirectly or directly, whom I thank.

My professors of communication at Ohio University taught me much about interpersonal communication. They provided a good foundation for organizing this book and analyzing the witnessing process, the ultimate communication transaction.

Dr. Henry and Mrs. Marie Einspruch, founders of The Lederer Foundation in Baltimore, Maryland, who provided literature that had a major impact on my life, and whose shoes I had the privilege of stepping into in 1988.

Dan and Arlene Rigney, whose love and patience enabled me to see the truth that the Messiah had come. Pat Klein, a terrific publishing consultant and friend, who gave me guidance as I wrote this book. Dr. Louis Goldberg, a friend for many years, and who willingly read and commented on my manuscript.

My wife, Steffi, who not only illustrated this book, capturing the content of each chapter in a cartoon, but also helped me find more effective ways of expressing my thoughts. She has been there for me ever since we married.

Rebecca and Shira, my lovely daughters, for just being themselves. Also, Rebecca contributed some excellent editing to the revised edition.

My parents, who brought me up with an appreciation of my Jewish heritage and an identification with my people. (All right, I admit it, they would have preferred me writing a different book and going into a different line of work.)

And, of course, I thank God and his Messiah, through whom I have been given eternal and abundant life.

INTRODUCTION

CATCHING FISH FOR THE MESSIAH

— or —

It's the Perfect Time to Drop Your Line

When I was a young boy, I saw a cartoon (Disney, I think) about fishing. One scene greatly impressed me. Each time the fisherman (Goofy, I think) tossed in his line, he landed a big one. Soon he had a pile of fish on the shore as tall as himself. "Wow, that looks like fun," I thought. Since there was a small lake in my little Maryland town, I decided to try my hand at fishing. It looked so easy!

Grabbing a broom handle and tying a string to the end of it, I marched down to the lake with determination and dropped in my line. After what seemed like days—probably an hour or two—I headed home, discouraged, dejected, and definitely finished with fishing . . . forever! I hadn't even gotten one nibble.

That evening my dad came home from work and found me sitting on the porch, head in hands.

"What's wrong?" he asked, reading my sad expression. I told him about my totally unproductive fishing expedition. Trying not to look too amused, my father questioned me about my fishing technique.

"What did you use for bait?" he asked.

"Bait?" I repeated. "What's bait?"

"It's what you put on the end of the hook to attract the fish."

"Oh," I said. "What's a hook?"

Apparently I had missed some of the finer fundamentals of fishing. I had seen that cartoon character catching fish, but must have missed what he had done to prepare to catch those fish. (Cartoons do take certain liberties with reality!)

Dad then explained about hooks and bait. Was I relieved to know that I didn't have to give up fishing forever!

When I speak in churches, invariably I'll hear stories about people's attempts to witness to Jewish people. These stories often remind me of that first fishing trip. In their zeal to "catch a fish," many people overlook the fundamentals. They give it a try but come home discouraged, dejected, definitely finished with "fishing."

I don't want that to happen to you. I want you to be effective in your witnessing so that you don't become discouraged. After all, how are my fellow Jews going to hear the Gospel if Gentile believers are too discouraged to share it with them? There aren't enough of us "professionals" to have a personal witness with all Jewish people. You have a very important role.

Yeshua promised to make his disciples "fishers of men." Although the fishing techniques of the first century—large nets—are vastly different from the techniques of Goofy and of today, each method requires a basic understanding of the fundamentals of its type of fishing in order to be effective.

Likewise, there are certain fundamentals you need to learn in order to effectively share the Gospel with Jewish people. That's the purpose of this book—to help you learn how to share with your neighbor, your fellow worker, or even a Jewish person who has married into your family.

To help you organize all the material you will be learning, I've included what I call a witnessing model. I used models when I taught college communications courses and have found them useful in the Jewish evangelism training programs I've taught.

This book is divided into four sections:

I. You: The Gentile Christian
II. Your Message: The "Jewish Gospel"
III. The Audience: Your Jewish Neighbor
IV. The Feedback: Barriers to Belief

Section I is about you, the Gentile Christian. This section will help you understand your role in Jewish evangelism. God has a very special challenge for you that, sad to say, the Church hasn't taken up very well over the centuries.

WITNESSING MODEL FOR JEWISH EVANGELISM

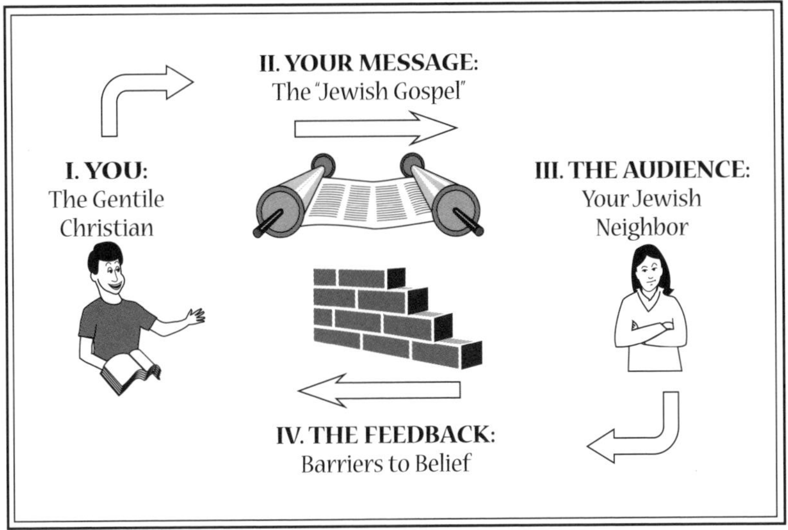

I share in Section II about the "Jewish Gospel." While it's true that there is only one Gospel of salvation for Jews and Gentiles, there are many ways of presenting it. Those involved with children's evangelism communicate the Gospel to little ones in a unique way. Those working with college students have outreach approaches that are effective on campuses. This same principle holds true for Jewish people. Section II will teach you how to share the Good News in a "Jewish" way.

Section III will help you better understand your Jewish neighbor. It would be foolish to imply that after reading a few pages in this book, you will really *know* your Jewish neighbor. That would not only be impossible, it would be presumptuous. Getting to know someone takes time. Nevertheless, a look into Jewish history, religion, and culture should offer you a greater understanding of the people to which your Jewish neighbor belongs.

The last section, Section IV, discusses the unique responses your Jewish neighbor might offer as you present the Gospel. Not only will we deal with the more common Jewish objections to the Gospel, but we will also look at questions that may not really be questions at all. We'll examine how to apply principles of discernment in your witness.

Let me encourage you. You couldn't have picked a better time to get involved in Jewish evangelism. Not since the first century have so many Jewish people come to believe in Yeshua. No one but God can give exact numbers, but I have seen estimates that there are more than 250,000 Jewish believers in the United States and twice as many worldwide.

In the former Soviet Union, many thousands have responded to the outreach efforts of Jewish ministries. In Israel, too, there are thousands of Jewish believers.

One visible evidence of the existence of these large numbers of Jewish believers is the rise in what has become known as the Messianic congregational movement. Whereas thirty years ago you might have found small pockets of Jewish believers meeting for weekly Bible study, today you can visit any of the hundreds of congregations where Jewish and Gentile believers in Yeshua worship God in a distinctively Jewish way.

There are Messianic congregations and fellowships all over the world. Messianic conferences attract many thousands interested in the Jewish expression of faith in Yeshua. And this "Messianic movement" is growing!

The impact of God's Spirit moving among Jewish people is underlined by the recent appearance of several groups who counter the witness of those they call "tricky missionaries." Misunderstanding the loving purpose of those who spread the Gospel, these groups suspect the motives of missionaries and warn the Jewish people away from their message. They accuse Jewish believers who maintain a Jewish identity of being deceptive, of using Jewish practices to mislead unsuspecting Jews. In fact, lately these groups have been saying that Jews who trust Yeshua *are no longer Jews*! We know that something is happening because the opposition is busy as well.

Now that you understand the structure of this book and see the very real possibilities for success, let me help you become a successful fisherman for the Messiah. Let's begin by taking a look at you, the Gentile Christian. You may be surprised by much of what I'm about to share with you. My prayer is that you'll also be challenged to act.

SECTION I

You: The Gentile Christian

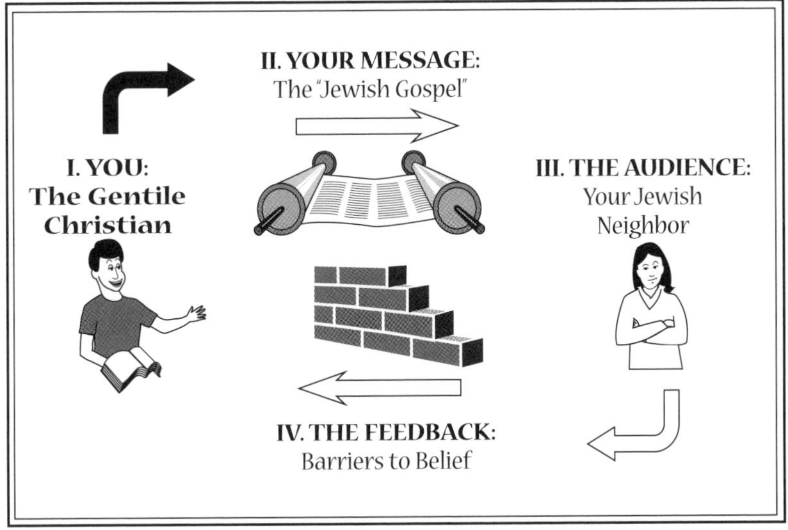

As you can see from our witnessing model, *you* begin the process. Some people think that reaching Jewish people is a job solely for the Jewish missionary. I don't think so. Non-professional Gentiles have a specific job to do in Jewish evangelism. Apparently you agree, or you wouldn't be reading this book.

Section I is all about you and how you fit into the plan for Israel's salvation. Chapter 1 discusses what God has said about the need to witness to his chosen people. It can help you appreciate the biblical basis for Jewish evangelism and how it fits into the plan of God.

In case you start to think,"Who, me, a Gentile, witness to a Jew?" I've included chapter 2 to encourage you. You'll see not only why Gentiles are often *more* effective witnessing to Jews, but also how God planned for you, a non-Jew, to be a part of the process of reaching Jewish people for Yeshua, the Messiah.

Everyone witnesses within a context. I've already shared with you that this is a very encouraging time to be talking to Jews about Yeshua. But realize, too, that this comes at the end of a 2,000-year drought. Chapter 3 reviews certain events of history that pertain to the "Church"* and her relationship with the Jewish people. Some of the story is not pretty. I'm not offering this information to instill guilt, but to make you aware, in case you're not, of some reasons Jewish people may hesitate to learn about Yeshua.

The last chapter of Section I offers some suggestions for becoming more credible in your testimony. It *is* the Word of God, delivered with much prayer, that wins souls. The truth is, however, that the message is inextricably linked to the messenger. As you will see later, the apostle Paul spoke about this very issue of credibility.

Let's now turn the spotlight on you, a Gentile believer in Yeshua, with a heartfelt desire to share the love of the Messiah with your Jewish neighbor. There are people and forces who will discourage you from your pursuit. The following chapter should help you stand firm in your conviction to witness to the lost sheep of the house of Israel.

---

* From time to time, you'll notice in the text that the words "Church" or "Christian" appear in quotation marks. This is to emphasize that there have been individuals who, though calling themselves Christians or identifying with the Church, have not always behaved like true followers of the Messiah. This is particularly noteworthy when it comes to certain historical events concerning the Jews. Therefore, the terms are confusing to many Jewish people. Throughout the book, then, when I refer to true followers of Yeshua (which, by the way, is how you say Jesus in Hebrew), I most often use the term "believer." As you will learn in Chapter 7, the words we use in our witness communicate differently to different people. I'm hoping you will become more sensitive to these issues.

— 1 —

SHOULD JEWS REALLY BE PERSUADED TO BELIEVE IN JESUS?

— or —

Should I Just Leave My Jewish Neighbor Alone?

Something strange is happening in several mainline Christian denominations. Theologians call it *liberalism*, getting away from the plain and simple Gospel message that Yeshua died to pay the debt for sin, and that by accepting his atoning work on our behalf we are granted eternal life.

Concurrent with this position, many leaders are steering their denominations and churches away from evangelizing Jewish people. They mean well, trying to be sensitive to those who have suffered centuries of prejudice and persecution in the name of "Christianity." But they do Jewish people eternal harm by withholding from them the Good News of the Messiah, Yeshua. Neglecting to present the message of salvation to the people for whom it was first intended is an unwitting, yet serious, act of anti-Semitism.

I know you don't agree with these church leaders. You picked up this book to learn more about sharing the Messiah with his people. But, because of the commitment of some *not* to share the Messiah with Jews, it's all the more important that you know why you should. In addition to the fact that Yeshua died to atone for the sins of all people, Jews as well as Gentiles, I'm now going to share with you four persuasive reasons to share the Messiah with Jewish people.

It Identifies Us With Our Spiritual Heroes

Growing up in Maryland, I looked forward to that first chill of autumn. It meant just one thing: football season! And, like other young boys, I had a hero. His name was Johnny Unitas, a quarterback for the then Baltimore Colts."Johnny U," as we called him, was perhaps the finest quarterback ever to play the game. Since I too, played that position, it was natural for me to identify with him. I wore his number—number 19. I tried to throw the ball the way he did. I even got a flat-top haircut to look like him. As much as I could, I tried to duplicate the details of my hero's life.

When winter thawed into spring, football drifted from my memory and baseball occupied my young mind. Now Mickey Mantle stood tall upon my hero's pedestal. Having spent my first and formative month of life in the Bronx, I naturally pledged my allegiance to the New York Yankees, the "Bronx Bombers." And back in the 1950s, "the Mick" was the man to emulate. Whatever the Mick did, that's what I longed to do.

Modeling ourselves after successful people is a way to grow into a successful life. Business people who want to get ahead read magazines like *Forbes* or *Fortune*. Individuals who want a more successful life go to self-improvement seminars and learn how the "winners" do it. Who would want an aerobics teacher who is fat and lumpy? If Richard Simmons gained weight, no one would be "sweatin' to the oldies" (or any music) with him. He'd stop being a good role model.

As we look through the Scriptures, we find something interesting about those who should be our spiritual role models. They had great concern for the salvation of the Jewish people.

Moses is a spiritual hero to many. Though he fell short of his ultimate goal of leading Israel *into* the promised land, he did lead them *to* it. And even though his people gave him plenty of *tsuris* (a Yiddish, or Jewish, word for "trouble"), he never lost the burden to rescue his people.

After the Israelites built a golden calf, directly disobeying the first of the Ten Commandments, Moses interceded with God on their behalf:

> Now, if you will just forgive their sin! But if you won't, then, I beg you, blot me out of your book which you have written!
>
> Exodus 32:32

Moses was willing to give up his life for this wayward, rebellious people.

The apostle Paul is also a well-known role model. While he states that he was the "apostle to the Gentiles," he, like Moses, had deep concern for his own people. In the midst of his doctrinal letter to the largely Gentile church at Rome, Paul was inspired to insert his feelings on this subject:

> My grief is so great, the pain in my heart so constant, that I could wish myself actually under God's curse and separated from the Messiah, if it would help my brothers, my own flesh and blood, the people of Israel! Romans 9:2–4

Believers in Yeshua have accepted him as the ultimate role model for spiritual growth. Paul taught that "those whom he knew in advance, he also determined in advance would be conformed to the pattern of his Son" (Romans 8:29). This pattern included a deep concern for his people, the Jews. Weeping over Jerusalem, Yeshua cried,

> Yerushalayim! Yerushalayim! You kill the prophets! You stone those who are sent to you! How often I wanted to gather your children, just as a hen gathers her chickens under her wings, but you refused! Matthew 23:37

This is only one of the many statements that reveals the Messiah's heart for his people. Even while dying on the cross, he extended his compassion to his confused, misdirected brethren and to the Romans who actually crucified him, saying, "Father, forgive them; they don't understand what they are doing" (Luke 23:34).

These examples show that Moses, Paul, and even Messiah Yeshua shared a common burden for the salvation of the Jewish people. All were willing to sacrifice themselves to accomplish that goal. If you want to be more like the heroes of Scripture, it means assuming their burden that many of the nation of Israel might receive God's forgiveness and love.

It's a Good Investment

Former *New York Times* reporter McCandlish Phillips, in his fascinating book *The Bible, The Supernatural, and The Jews* states boldly:

> Jews are socially and culturally influential. They cannot avoid being influential as a people. In any society in which they are found, Jews are influential out of proportion to their numbers. They affect the history of the nation they are in and they affect its culture. To a significant extent the history and culture of the nation will turn on what some Jews do. It is written into the very nature of the Jews, by the finger of God, to be influential (p. 279).

A second reason for sharing the Gospel with Jewish people is that it is a sound investment of time and love. Why? Because of the God-given zeal of the Jewish people.

Consider the enormous impact individual Jews have had on history. For a people of such small numbers, the impact *is* disproportionate. Phillips reminds us of Moses, Yeshua, Marx, Freud and Einstein. He states that "such Jews have had a vast impact and influence on the affairs of mankind." According to M. Hirsch Goldberg, in his entertaining and enlightening book *The Jewish Connection,* explains that,

> Mark Twain, surveying the wide-ranging activity of Jews in his day, once cracked that there must be at least 25 million Jews living in America. Of course, at no time during Twain's life were there more than 2 million Jews in the country. Twain, generally friendly to Jews, was simply expressing a feeling shared by friend and foe alike—Jews just seem to be all over (p. 107).

(Twain also pointed out that the mere existence of the Jews as an intact people is convincing proof of the existence of God!)

Have things changed much since Mark Twain penned his remarks? Not really. Jews still influence the world around them. In politics—Henry Kissinger to Madeline Albright (who recently discovered she was Jewish). In music—Leonard Bernstein to Josh Groban. In sports—Howard Cosell to baseball commissioner David Stern. In TV—George Burns to Jerry Seinfeld. In film—Paul Newman to Adam Sandler.

This disproportionate influence, which is not limited to the above examples or categories, is something that the apostle Paul described in Romans 10:1–2:

> Brothers, my heart's deepest desire and my prayer to God for Israel is for their salvation; for I can testify to their zeal for God. But it is not based on correct understanding. . . .

This zeal, this influence, was given to the Jewish people by God to bring blessing to the entire world. That's what he promised to Abram: "by you all the families of the earth will be blessed" (Genesis 12:3).

It was a blessing to the world that two Jews, Jonah Salk and Albert Sabin, conquered polio. It's been a blessing to enjoy the comedic and dramatic talents of Milton Berle, Jerry Lewis, and Dustin Hoffman. And who wouldn't agree that, after a hard day's work, it's a blessing to come home and slip into your most comfortable pair of Levis (as in Levi Strauss) or Calvins (as in Calvin Klein)?

Think of all the constructive, helpful, and charitable contributions that Jews have made—in medicine, in music, in movies, in science, in literature, in art, in scholarship. God-given talent combined with God-given zeal have indeed worked together for the good of all mankind. Imagine what a blessing it will be to the Kingdom of God when this talent becomes devoted directly to God and the Messiah!

The Jews of Yeshua's day, much like Orthodox Jews today, had a tremendous zeal for God, but their zeal was not according to complete biblical revelation. Most Jewish people, then as now, have unfortunately missed the Messiah. Paul wrote:

> For, since they are unaware of God's way of making people righteous and instead seek to set up their own, they have not

submitted themselves to God's way of making people righteous. Romans 10:3

This attempt to attain righteousness through good works can be seen more clearly on the Jewish High Holy Days than at any other time of the year. Jewish people flock to synagogues, hoping, through their attendance and recited prayers, to achieve atonement for their sins, though the Temple has been destroyed, and with it, the sacrificial system. Even though these holy days do cause my people to consider their ways, that's not enough. It may clear the conscience, but it does not cleanse the soul. Only Yeshua's sacrifice can do that.

The intensity of the holiday season is what might be called "misdirected zeal." Focused on the needs of the world, this fervor brings blessing to the world. When this God-given passion is turned against God, it causes problems. Karl Marx, author of *The Communist Manifesto*, was a Jew promoting an atheistic way of life as part of Communism. However, when zeal is directed toward God, it brings blessing to the people of God.

The enthusiasm that was built into the Jews by God often finds expression in some very non-Jewish and not particularly biblical activities. My own "misdirected zeal" led me down a confusing and dangerous path before God set my feet on solid ground.

Since I was not a very religious Jew, I was not particularly concerned with keeping the laws and traditions of my people; I leveled my sights toward the lofty pursuit of "Truth." I spent my young adult life engrossed in psychology, philosophy, and the study of the religions of the world. Finally, I was initiated into the newly packaged, ancient art of Transcendental Meditation, or T.M., a disguised form of Hinduism.

T.M. is a movement which was popularized by the Maharishi Mahesh Yogi, a man who gained renown when the Beatles subscribed to his teachings. This "guru" brought T.M. to the Western world. Packaged as a technique for relaxation, T.M. promised to enable people to achieve their highest human potential.

It was the late 1960s. Tensions in the United States ran high. Students actively protested a war in Vietnam. Drugs and divorce were epidemic. Blacks and whites struggled with the issue of racial equality and civil rights.

Living in Washington, D.C., I felt a unique kind of tension all around me. The racial conflict found expression on the campus where I was teaching, Howard University, a predominantly black university; my parents and the parents of many of my friends were getting divorced; regular "peace" marches took place not far from where I lived. A "simple technique to relieve stress and strain" (another pitch of T.M.) sounded like just what the doctor ordered.

Furthermore, the prospect of achieving my full human potential also appealed to me. This had become a personal goal, something I believed everyone should strive for.

So with customary Jewish zeal, I dove into the practice of Transcendental Meditation, becoming convinced early on that the salvation of the world depended upon everyone meditating according to the tenets of T.M. So convinced was I that I enrolled in the teacher-training program so I could "save" the world.

I should have noticed what I was getting into from the beginning. The initiation ceremony included presenting an offering of fruit, flowers, and incense to the gods of Hinduism. There was also the fee of $75, the price of finding "god" at that time. (Inflation has driven the price substantially higher now, I am told.)

I should have become wary when, in the teacher-training program, the Maharishi expounded the Hindu scriptures. I should have noticed that my supposedly "unique" *mantra* (the sound I repeated over and over to help me meditate) was the same sound received by many others.

My eyes should have been opened when I heard of meditators having mental breakdowns during long meditation courses. And when I began to become more and more self-absorbed, I should have recognized that T.M. was antithetical to the Bible's message of love. But, as I will explain later, it wasn't until God himself broke through that I discovered that my misdirected zeal was dangerous to me and others.

I discovered that the second-in-command to the Maharishi was a Jewish man, like Joseph in Pharaoh's court and Mordecai in the government of Ahasuerus.

It is also rather amazing that thousands of other Jewish people—"seekers of truth," as we were called—joined me as we headed toward a religion totally foreign and diametrically opposed to the faith of our fathers.

The apostle Paul, discussing Jewish unbelief, said,

> Moreover, if their [the Jews'] stumbling is bringing riches to the world—that is, if Israel's being placed temporarily in a condition less favored than that of the Gentiles is bringing riches to the latter—how much greater riches will Israel in its fullness bring them! Romans 11:12

What I think he meant is just what I've been discussing here. Redirecting this God-given zeal, focusing it toward the work of God—especially the proclamation of the Gospel—is a potentially powerful tool for blessing! This, after all, was the task for which the Jews were originally created and to which we were initially called. And according to Revelation 7:4, it's exactly what 144,000 Jewish people will be doing sometime in the not-too-distant future!

God gave the Jews zeal, a supernaturally bestowed drive and enthusiasm, to bless the entire world. In many aspects of our lives, Jewish people have indeed been a blessing. But how much greater the blessing will be when this zeal, this drive, this intensity, is given to the purposes for which God initially intended it—to bring light to the nations, to declare the testimony of a faithful living God, to share with the world the love of the Messiah.

Reaching out to Jewish people can be a great investment. Think of how redirecting that Jewish zeal might change the world for God.

It Will Get Results

A theme runs through Scripture that is often untaught—the remnant. The remnant concept explains why some people seek God and choose to follow his ways, and why others do not. Because this remnant exists today among the Jews, we have God's guarantee that our witnessing will produce results.

You could say that the remnant began back in the Garden of Eden. Abel was part of the remnant; Cain was not. Later, Isaac was part of the remnant; Ishmael was not. Jacob was; Esau was not. The list goes on.

In Romans 11, Paul introduced the remnant theme in his argument for Jewish evangelism. He asked rhetorically,

> In that case, I say, isn't it that God has repudiated his people [because Gentiles believe]? Heaven forbid! For I myself am a son of Israel, from the seed of Avraham [Abraham], of the tribe of Binyamin [Benjamin]. God has not repudiated his people, whom he chose in advance. Or don't you know what the *Tanakh* [Old Testament] says about Eliyahu [Elijah]? He pleads with God against Israel, "Adonai, they have killed your prophets and torn down your altars, and I'm the only one left, and now they want to kill me too!" But what is God's answer to him? "I have kept for myself seven thousand men who have not knelt down to Ba'al." It's the same way in the present age: there is a remnant, chosen by grace.
>
> Romans 11:1-5

Paul referred to 7,000 faithful believers in the days of Elijah who stood for God, and he went on to say that there was a remnant in his day, too.

There is *still* a remnant!

Not since the first century have so many Jews come to believe that Yeshua is the promised Messiah. In addition to the hundreds of Messianic congregations in this country that I have already mentioned, there are also thousands of Jewish people who attend traditional churches. As I said earlier, estimates range from 200,000 to 300,000. This number may not seem to be a large percentage of the total current U.S. Jewish population of about six million. But a remnant is just that—a remnant. And the remnant is growing.

Only a few decades ago, those who worked in the field of Jewish evangelism harvested little fruit. Undaunted by the slow response, they believed what they could not see—that there was a remnant waiting to respond. Today, in part because of their faithfulness, the work of witnessing to Jewish people is being blessed with abundant reward. Seed sown in the past is producing ripe fruit and much of it is ready for harvesting.

There are times when I have shared the message of the Messiah with Jewish people and received immediate results. Recently it was with a seventy-six-year-old Jewish lady who just needed a little nudge in order to profess her faith. Another time it was with a young man who came to our congregation. Like the Philippian jailer in Acts 16, he asked, "What must I do to be saved?"

This means it is entirely possible that *your* neighbor, co-worker, or friend might be part of the remnant, waiting to respond to the Good News. If you learn to communicate the message of the Messiah effectively, you can be the one to bring God's blessing to one of his chosen people.

It Will Reap a Reward from God

I don't know why he does it, but the Bible makes it clear that God blesses those who bless the Jews. There is an unusual promise in Genesis, first given to Abram, the father of the Jewish people: "I will bless those who bless you, but I will curse anyone who curses you" (Genesis 12:3). Scripture has proved the truth of this unique promise many times. And it's true for our times as well.

Abraham's son Isaac settled in Gerar, the land of Abimelech, king of the Philistines. There was no love lost between Abimelech's people and the family of Abraham. Yet, when Abimelech saw how God made Isaac prosper, in spite of the Philistines' hostility toward him, Abimelech went to Isaac and said:

> We saw very clearly that *Adonai* has been with you; so we said,

> "Let there be an oath between us: let's make a pact between ourselves and you that you will not harm us, just as we have not caused you any offense but have done you nothing but good and sent you on your way in peace. Now *you are blessed by* ADONAI." Genesis 26:28–29, emphasis mine

Bad blood or no, Abimelech did not want to be on the wrong side of God.

As he was dying, Isaac repeated God's promise to his son Jacob: "Cursed be everyone who curses you, and blessed be everyone who blesses you!" (Genesis 27:29) Even though Isaac did not know which son he was blessing, it is clear that he wanted to reiterate God's promise that it is better to bless the Jewish people than to curse them.

This warning held true throughout the Bible. The Egyptian Pharaoh who enslaved the Israelites was a classic case of someone who "passed over" getting blessed and got cursed instead. He would not allow the Israelites to take a three-day journey into the wilderness to worship God, and what did he get? A bloody Nile, frogs galore, lice, insects, diseased livestock, boils, hail, locusts, darkness, and the death of all the firstborn of Egypt. Finally, he lost all his good workers when the exodus of the Israelites took place and, to make matters worse, his own army was destroyed. It would have been better for him to get God's message about blessing the Jews in the first place.

Rahab the harlot was a lot smarter than Pharaoh when it came to blessing and cursing. She told the Israelites who had come to spy on her city of Jericho,

> I know that *ADONAI* has given you the land. . . . We've heard how *ADONAI* dried up the water in the Sea of Suf [Red Sea] ahead of you. . . . For *ADONAI* your God—he is God in heaven above and on earth below. So, please, swear to me by *ADONAI* that, since I have been kind to you, you will also be kind to my father's family. Joshua 2:9–12

Unlike Pharaoh, this prostitute was not too proud to pay attention to God.

By far the best example of blessing for blessing and cursing for cursing is found in the book of Esther. It is set in the Medo-Persian Empire while the Jews were in captivity and Haman was prime minister under King Ahasuerus (Xerxes). Incensed when Mordecai, a Jew, would not bow down to him, Haman had a 75-foot gallows built for the sheer pleasure of watching this "rebel" hang. And to top it off, he got the king to sign into law a decree ordering the death of all Jews. As the book of Esther records, because of Haman's desire to punish the Jews, God reversed the curse (Esther 7:10). It was Haman who swung from the end of his own rope.

Where are the mighty peoples who mistreated the Jewish people through the ages? The Roman Empire? The Ottomans? The Nazis? A country-by-country tally would show the rise and fall of those who dared touch the apple of God's eye. But, since ancient times, the existence and blessing of the Jewish people remain a testimony to the faithfulness of God.

Matthew 25:31–40 reports Yeshua's message about the final blessing at the end of this age. When the Son of Man returns, he will gather all nations before him and separate them the way a herdsman separates sheep from goats. The basis for this separation will be the treatment the nations gave Yeshua. Did they feed him when he was hungry? Did they clothe him when he was naked? Did they visit him in prison?

The righteous ones will be confused:

> Lord, when did we see you hungry, and feed you, or thirsty and give you something to drink? When did we see you a stranger and make you our guest, or needing clothes and provide them? When did we see you sick or in prison, and visit you? Matthew 25:37–39

Yeshua will explain that his identification with his people is so total that behavior toward them is experienced in a very personal way.

> The King will say to them, "Yes! I tell you that whenever you did these things for one of the least important of these

brothers of mine, you did them for me!" Matthew 25:40

Some interpret the expression "these brothers of mine" to be referring exclusively to Christians. I've even heard that it refers to children, because the phrase "least important" is used to describe these "brothers." But given the "blessing/cursing" concept so well established in Scripture, and the context of the passage, it seems to me that it is the Jews that the Messiah is specifically referring to. Remember, although Messiah did die for *all* people, he had a particular burden for his own flesh-and-blood brothers. Surely, he would not suddenly change his father's policy on how to treat the chosen people.

In 1980 I had the privilege of preaching in one of those California mega-churches. As is my general custom, I asked the pastor how things were going in his congregation. I was particularly interested in knowing what he believed was responsible for such incredible growth!

"Barry," he confessed, "we were always operating in the red, spending more than we took in. It wasn't until I made a commitment to follow the scriptural admonition to care for Yeshua's brethren that the Lord began to bless us. Ever since we began to invite a Jewish missionary to address us at the beginning of each year and to support Jewish missions, we have been operating in the black, *never once* showing a deficit. That's why we've got you here on this first Sunday in January!" This is more evidence that God keeps his promise to bless those who bless the Jews.

God, *whatever* his purposes were, chose to use the Jews as a test. My people were not chosen because we were better than anyone else. Rather, we were chosen to exhibit to the world the grace and faithfulness of God. As it is written,

> For you are a people set apart as holy for *Adonai* your God. *Adonai* your God has chosen you out of all the peoples on the face of the earth to be his own unique treasure.
>
> Deuteronomy 7:6

God cares greatly for his chosen people, so much so that he

was willing to sacrifice the best Jew who ever lived to make atonement. If God would do this much for his people, it follows that he would shower great blessings on those who love and care for them as well. That is his will.

Remember the margarine commercial that said, "Don't mess with Mother Nature"? An even truer statement is "Don't mess with Father God, *or* with his chosen children."

As I said earlier, there is much opposition to telling Jewish people about the Messiah. At times when you encounter resistance, when your best intentions meet with rebuff, that's when you'll want to recall all that God has promised to those who bring blessings to Jews, especially the greatest blessing of all—salvation.

You'll want to keep in mind that caring for the Jewish people was a hallmark of the heroes of our faith. Remember that bringing Jewish people into the Kingdom is a good investment for eternity. Remember that your neighbor might be part of the remnant. And, finally, keep in mind that God promised to bless you if you will bless your Jewish friend by introducing him or her to the Messiah.

Now that this is clear in your mind, let me anticipate a question you may have. I hear it often when I speak in churches:

"O.K. I want to see Jewish people saved, but isn't that the work of other Jews and professional missionaries to the Jews? Can I, an untrained Gentile, really play a role in telling Jewish people about Yeshua?"

My unequivocal answer to you is *YES!*

— 2 —

GENTILES CAN PLAY A PART IN JEWISH EVANGELISM!

— or —

Provoke 'em to Jealousy!

During the late 1960s I was faced with a tough decision. The Vietnam War was raging. The draft lottery was operating. My number was low. So I decided to fulfill my military obligation by joining the United States Coast Guard Reserves. After six months of active duty, I was assigned to a Reserve Unit in Washington, D.C., committing me to serve one weekend a month.

One of the most distasteful tasks I had to perform was "swabbing the deck." It wasn't that the work was so hard, but the floor had just been cleaned by the "regulars" before their weekend leave. I felt indignant that I had to clean a perfectly clean floor. Clearly, this was just busywork.

One of my buddies shared this boring job with me, but it was obvious that he did not share my bad attitude toward it. While I mumbled and grumbled, moaned and groaned, my buddy Loren had the *chutzpah* (Yiddish for "nerve") to whistle and sing! It drove me crazy. After all, wasn't I the one who, through Transcendental Meditation, was supposedly learning to achieve inner peace and relaxation?

One day I had had enough.

"Loren," I said, "what is it about you that makes you so blankety-blank happy?" My language had become somewhat salty in my six months of active duty.

Loren's response was simple, but it changed my life. Smiling, he said, "Your Messiah lives in my heart!"

"My Messiah? What's *my* Messiah doing in *your* heart?" I yelled in a not-too-peaceful manner. Then I thought a moment. "And besides," I added, "who *is* my Messiah?"

Loren explained to me that Yeshua was the Messiah, sent first to my people, the Jews. If I accepted him into my life, I would find peace. Real peace!

I was jealous. He seemed to have something real, something worthwhile. Whatever it was, I certainly was not getting it through T.M. And although I wasn't about to make a decision about Jesus without some serious study, Loren had planted a seed of desire within my soul. That desire eventually found fulfillment in Jesus, Yeshua, the Messiah.

In Romans, Paul asks rhetorically,

> In that case, I say, isn't it that they [the Jews] stumbled with the result that they have permanently fallen away? Heaven forbid! Quite the contrary, it is by means of their stumbling that the deliverance has come to the Gentiles, *in order to provoke them to jealousy.*
>
> Romans 11:11, emphasis mine

In the *Torah*, the five books of Moses, the Lord told Israel that he would "arouse their jealousy with a non-people" (Deuteronomy 32:21). Paul quoted this verse in Romans 10:19 to explain God's approach for reaching his people. He would accomplish this through the nations, the Gentiles.

It came true in my life as it has in the lives of many Jewish people who have received the Messiah through the testimony of a non-Jewish believer. Many have been "provoked to jealousy" by a people who are not even a people.

You're familiar with Matthew 28:19, commonly called the Great Commission: "Therefore, go and make people from all nations into *talmidim* [Hebrew for students or disciples], immersing them into the reality of the Father, the Son and the *Ruach HaKodesh* [Holy Spirit]." This verse is appropriate and motivational to quote when missionaries are sent on the mission field. But remember, this Commission was not spoken to Gentiles. It was given by Jesus to a handful of Jews.

They were told to fulfill their calling as Jews. Beginning in Jerusalem (Luke 24:47) they were to share the message first with the Jews, and then with all the nations of the world, that is, the Gentiles, and make disciples out of them. And since you are most likely reading this book somewhere outside of Jerusalem, we can safely assume that the work those Jewish *sh'lichim* (Hebrew for apostles) began nearly 2,000 years ago has indeed been effective.

The Great Commission was given directly to Jews, but I believe God has a commission for Gentiles as well, one that many Gentiles who witness to Jewish people have used effectively. I call it "the Gentile Great Commission." You've just been reading about it: "provoke the Jews to jealousy!"

About this time you might be asking yourself, "Isn't making people jealous a pretty nasty way for a believer to behave?" Perhaps it just doesn't sound right to you. But Paul wasn't suggesting that you adopt a "holier-than-thou," or condescending attitude. He wasn't advising Gentiles to put on airs or act superior toward Jews. In fact, he spoke to the congregation at Rome about the importance of having a proper perspective toward Jews:

> Moreover, if their stumbling is bringing riches to the world—that is, if Israel's being placed temporarily in a condition less favored than that of the Gentiles is bringing riches to the latter—how much greater riches will Israel in its fullness bring them!
> Romans 11:12

Paul is commenting on the fact that the transgression, or turning away, of the Jewish people from the Gospel hastened the arrival of the Gospel to the Gentiles. Paul told his Jewish hearers, for instance, "It was necessary that God's word be spoken first to you [the Jews]. But since you are rejecting it . . . we're turning to the *Goyim* [Gentiles]!" (Acts 13:46) If this transgression by the Jews, therefore, meant life for the Gentiles, how much more the world will be blessed in the fulfillment, when Jews do come to believe.

In other words, believers should look forward to the day when the Jewish people will experience fulfillment in the Messiah. What a blessing it will be when Messiah's body is once again brimming with Jews like it was at the start!

In his discussion of the olive tree in Romans 11, Paul further cautioned the congregation at Rome to regard the unbelieving Jewish people with a proper attitude. He described all Jewish people as the natural branches of an olive tree and the Gentiles as wild branches.

Remember that "in the first place, the Jews were entrusted with the very words of God" (Romans 3:2); the Gentiles were pagans for the most part, worshiping idols, sacrificing children, practicing ungodly rituals, and believing a host of superstitions. Then, at their acceptance of the Messiah, Gentiles were "grafted in" among the natural branches of the olive tree.

Paul warned the Gentile believers that even though they were now part of the tree, and even though some natural branches had been broken off because of unbelief (Romans 11:20), the Gentiles in the "body" were not to consider themselves superior to Jews who did not yet believe. Those Jews still represented the "root" of the tree which God had cultivated for almost 2,000 years. Paul told them:

> then don't boast as if you were better than the branches! However, if you do boast, remember that you are not supporting the root, the root is supporting you. . . . For if you were cut out of what is by nature a wild olive tree and grafted, contrary to nature, into a cultivated olive tree, how much more will these natural branches be grafted into their own olive tree!
>
> Romans 11:18, 24

Paul's purpose was to teach Gentiles the proper attitude. God never "unchose" his chosen people. Even when they disobeyed him—as they often did—he still cherished them as his own, amid the chastisement, and sought to lead them to repent. "For God's free gifts and his calling are irrevocable" (Romans 11:29).

Elsewhere Paul wrote of the Jewish people:

> . . .They were made God's children, the *Sh'khinah* [manifest presence of God] has been with them, the covenants are theirs, likewise the giving of the *Torah*, the Temple service and the promises; the Patriarchs are theirs; and from them, as far as his physical descent is concerned, came the Messiah, who is over all.
>
> Romans 9:4-5

The blessing of Jewish heritage and the calling to carry out God's purpose has never changed. The gifts with which God has equipped his people for his purpose have contributed to the good of the whole world.

With an attitude of humility and gratitude in order to provoke godly jealousy, you, a Gentile, may have an even more effective witness to Jewish people than many Jewish believers. You can cause your Jewish neighbor to long for the peace and inner happiness you have. I know it worked to draw me to Messiah. It will work with others, too.

— 3 —

ANTI-SEMITISM AND THE CHURCH

— or —

"Christians" Are Not Always Friendly Neighbors

Jewish people almost *expect* believers to try to evangelize them. Jews know about Billy Graham, having occasionally bumped into one of his crusades while watching TV. Evangelism is seen as expected behavior for a Christian, so offense is not always taken.

However, you must keep in mind the horrendous history of "Christian"-Jewish relations. It is difficult for Jewish people to distinguish the real Jesus through a filter of nearly 2,000 years of persecution against Jews in his name.

This chapter will review, briefly, some of the horrors which have happened to God's chosen people "in the name" of Jesus. It is not my intention to place a "guilt trip" on the Church. Nor am I implying that the twentieth-century Christian is responsible for the atrocities perpetrated on Jews by those who may not have been practicing Christian love. Rather, I want you to become familiar with the poor track record of "Christian"- Jewish relations in order to help you appreciate the defensive posture your Jewish friend might assume as you attempt to assure him or her of the love of Yeshua the Messiah.

The small town in Maryland where I grew up was a microcosm of the entire United States. We had a Little League for us youthful baseball players. There was a community pool. Everyone attended the dazzling Fourth of July celebrations. While some cities tend to form natural boundaries dividing the black neighborhood from the Italian section, or the Irish block from the Jewish area, our town was a spicy potpourri, a mixture of all kinds of people co-existing peacefully.

Because of this unusual blend, many of my friends were non-Jews. Some were Protestants, some were Catholics. It never seemed to matter much. What was really important was who hit the baseball the farthest!

Until my *Bar Mitzvah*.

Jewish boys, at the age of thirteen, go through a ceremony known as *Bar Mitzvah*, literally "Son of the Commandment." We stand before our synagogues, read from the Scripture, give speeches, and assume our positions as "adults" in the Jewish community. A *Bar Mitzvah* is no small thing; it requires years of preparation.

Several days a week, prior to the date of my *Bar Mitzvah*, I had to leave baseball practice early in order to spend time with the rabbi—to study Hebrew, to compose and rehearse my speech, to prepare to chant my assigned portion of the Scripture. My friends didn't appreciate the significance of this important rite and they let their resentment show. It gave me my first taste of anti-Semitism.

It was hard for me to believe, but one June afternoon, my best friend, Kenny, began to taunt me in front of the other guys, "Barry's going to 'Heeb-Jew' lessons." His words stung. There was derision in his voice. Other boys began to murmur that their dads had told them we Jews had killed Christ. It was the most unpleasant moment in my life.

That kind of prejudice is the residue of two millennia of "Christian" anti-Semitism. Anti-Semitism that would make any true believer in Jesus sick! Sadly, you, as a Christian, stand in the shadow of those ugly events.

Later we will discuss what you can do to defuse some of the tension that has arisen between Jews and "Christians." Remember, I bring up this history now to help you understand what is often in the back of the mind of your Jewish friend when he or she starts to hear about the love of Jesus the Christ, Yeshua the Messiah.

The Jews and the Roman Empire

How would you feel if you were informed that you could no longer salute the American flag? If you were forbidden to have a Christmas tree? If the opinions expressed in your Bible commentaries were publicly denigrated and those books burned? If you were no longer allowed to worship God as you chose?

And how would you feel about those who enforced these restrictions?

This is not a make-believe scenario. These were the kinds of laws enacted and enforced against the Jews by the Roman government and later the Roman Catholic Church.

When the true Church began, nearly all of its members were Jews. They didn't see themselves as starting a new religion. In fact, they could hardly figure out what to do with the Gentiles who wanted to join in the worship of the Messiah.

The Acts of the Apostles (15:2) records "no small measure of discord and dispute" concerning those who were turning to Yeshua from among the Gentiles. Known as the Jerusalem Council, the leaders of the early Church hotly debated whether or not Gentiles who believed in Jesus had to follow the Law of Moses and be circumcised. This concern certainly underscores the Jewishness of the early Church.

But as time passed, Jewish believers became more and more separated from the Jewish community. When the believers fled Jerusalem before the destruction of the Temple, heeding the prophetic warnings of Yeshua, the split was emphasized. At the Council of Yavneh, which met near the end of the first century, a malediction concerning the "sectarians," including the Jewish believers in Jesus, was written. It was a prayer for the disappearance of these Jews from the synagogue. Then, in 134 C.E.,* Jewish believers opposed their Jewish leaders by refusing to participate in the Bar Kokhba revolt because this military leader was hailed as the Messiah.

The split became a chasm. Jewish believers in Yeshua, seen as traitors,

* Instead of using the initials A.D., which stand for the Latin *Anno Domini*, "year of our Lord," I have chosen to use C.E., standing for "Common Era," as Jews refer to this same period. I will use B.C.E., "Before the Common Era," instead of B.C., "Before Christ," for dates before the Messiah was born. This will sensitize you toward talking with Jewish people.

were further separated from the fellowship of the Jewish community.

As this separation between the believers and the Jewish community widened, Rome began to restrict Jewish forms of worship and identity. Those in the Jewish community were called "superstitious" because they believed in a God they could not see. They were also labeled as haters of humanity when they would not participate in pagan practices which were so prevalent in the Roman Empire. Since much of the public celebration in Rome was imbued with religious significance, Jews were also called unpatriotic because they would not join in. For example, in Egypt, which was part of the Roman Empire, the story of God's judgment upon Pharaoh was changed. It was said that Jews were lepers who had been expelled from Egypt, not chosen people who had been delivered by God.

A tremendous struggle ensued between Judaism, that is, the way of life of the Jews, and Hellenism, the way of life of the Romans (and their predecessors, the Greeks). In order to do away with the Jewish people as a distinct entity, the emperor, Hadrian, forbade circumcision, Sabbath observance, Jewish holidays, rabbinical academies, study of *Torah* (the five books of Moses), and more.

Even though the Romans discouraged the practice of Judaism, somehow the Jews remained intact as a people.

You will hear that it was the study of *Torah* and *Talmud* (the codified writings of the rabbis) that kept the Jewish people together. Perhaps God used this, for in an almost miraculous way, the Roman emperor Vespasian permitted Yochanan ben Zakkai, a famous Pharisee of the first century, to start a seminary in Yavneh, which later became the center of Jewish learning. That education did indeed help the Jews stay a people.

During the early rule of the Roman Empire, there was a separation between the Jewish believers and the Jewish community, and pressure on all Jews to adopt the Roman way of life. This laid the foundation for the anti-Jewish attitudes seen in the next centuries.

It should be noted that there were many Jewish believers living in the Roman Empire, as well as many Jewish unbelievers, during this period. Many of the Jewish believers were prominent church leaders.

The Jews and Later Roman Rule

Many Gentiles living in the Roman Empire adopted "Christianity" when the Emperor Constantine (306-337) declared it to be the state religion. Few in the Church objected to the new anti-Semitic traditions Constantine instituted. By the 400s, Jews could no longer seek converts. Jews could not have non-Jewish slaves. The "Church" forbade intermarriage and in fact discouraged any contact between Christians and Jews. Some of the Church leaders, ostensibly followers of the Jew, Jesus, began to preach against the Jewish people.

These actions met with little Church resistance since one of the second-century Church fathers, Justin Martyr, had already laid the foundation for anti-Semitism. He had accused the Jews of inciting Romans to kill Christians. Origen, who died in 251 C.E., accused the Jews of plotting to murder Christians. Even John Chrysostom (344–407 C.E.), known as "the bishop with the golden tongue," called the Jews worthless, greedy, assassins of Christ, and worshipers of the devil. He stated from the pulpit that there could never be forgiveness for the Jews and that it was "incumbent" on Christians to hate them. Jerome, a contemporary of Chrysostom and translator of the Latin Vulgate, devoted one of his celebrated essays entirely to the Jews. Ironic that he had learned Hebrew from a rabbi.

With that kind of ecclesiastical support, other anti-Jewish changes were made. Sunday, the day that commemorated the Resurrection, became the Sabbath day. Passover became Easter, taking the name of a pagan goddess, Ishtar. Fertility rites soon clouded the truth of the Resurrection. In general, what was then known as Christianity ignored the Jewish people, except to persecute them.

The Roman Catholic Church saw itself as the new Israel and, therefore, the new "chosen people." Presumably to rid itself of potential "competition," it prohibited many Jewish customs. Observance of Passover was forbidden. The reading of the *Talmud* was outlawed, and priceless, hand-copied works were burned. Invoking the new laws of the Roman government, the state church did all it could to destroy the identity of the Jews, driving God's people further and further away from the Messiah.

The Jews and the Second Millennium

Everyone has heard of the Crusades.

In the eleventh and twelfth centuries, a new program was carried out, begun under orders of Pope Urban II. He promised forgiveness and guaranteed entrance to Paradise to those "Christians" who participated in his plan. Under it, thousands of Crusaders, children included, marched to the Holy Land to deliver it from the infidels, the Muslims who lived there.

The intention of the Crusaders was to drive the Mohammedans from the sacred soil of Yeshua's homeland. In their religious zeal, they enlisted many not-so-religious people, fortune-hunters, people of low standing looking for some adventure, serfs looking for freedom.

Picture a long parade of soldiers, faces set with determination, prepared for "holy battle." And what do they carry for their standard? The cross, symbol of loyalty to their Lord.

Tragically for the Jews, the Crusaders decided they could start defending "Christianity" right at home. They didn't have to go all the way to Israel to get rid of infidels. Jews, people who opposed what they understood to be "Christianity," lived right there among them. Soon, "Kill a Jew and save your soul!" became the battle cry of the zealous Crusaders.

Later, when the Crusaders arrived in Israel, armed with indignation leveled sharply at Jewish unbelief, the Crusaders rounded up the Jews in Jerusalem, herded them into a synagogue, and burned the building to the ground. Marching triumphantly around the inferno, they sang a hymn of praise to God—"Christ, We adore Thee." Inside the burning synagogue, Jews heard these strains of "Christian" worship as they perished.

It didn't get much better in the Roman Catholic Middle Ages. As frequently happened to the Jews, they were not allowed certain privileges, particularly the privilege of owning land or pursuing certain professions. Because of this, Jews often held unpopular professions, such as tax-collecting. The stereotype of the money-grabbing Jew was being etched into history.

Further, Jews were accused of causing many of the ills that befell the people of this age. They were held responsible for the Black Death, or Black Plague, of 1348, which killed a huge portion of Europe's population. It was rumored that Jews poisoned the wells. The Jews were also accused of causing many natural disasters, like the Lisbon earthquake. They were even charged with killing "Christian" children to get blood for *matzah*, the unleavened bread of Passover. The Roman Catholic Church laid the death of Messiah upon Jews for all time, eternally charging them with deicide. That accusation has only recently been renounced.

In the 1400s, the Catholic Church tried another approach in dealing with the Jews. The Jewish population of Spain was offered a choice: convert to Catholicism or die. Many chose to die rather than follow those they held as responsible for the deaths and destruction of so many other Jews.

The Spanish Inquisition remains another indelible black mark on the history of the Church and an enormous roadblock between the Jewish people and the person of Yeshua. To this day, during the holy day of *Yom Kippur*, the Day of Atonement, Jews chant a special prayer dating back to that time. It is a lament called *Kol Nidrey*, "All Vows." It was inserted in the liturgy of *Yom Kippur* because of the Spanish Inquisition. *Kol Nidrey* became a cry to nullify the confessions of "Christian" faith uttered by those who had claimed conversion to Catholicism under duress.

I wish I could say that in the Protestant Reformation anti-Semitism disappeared, but that is not the case.

Martin Luther, the great reformer, although first expressing great respect for the Jews, turned against them in his later years. Frustrated by the lack of Jewish conversions, he wrote that the root of their resistance to the Gospel was their evil nature. He accused the Jews of being ritual murderers, incapable of being saved. He urged the destruction of all Jewish synagogues as well as religious books such as the *Talmud*. Toward the end of his life, he said that since Jews would not convert, "We ought not to suffer them or bear with them any longer." It is true that he later repented of many of his statements against the Jews, but once before the public, those words were used against the nation of Israel again and again.

The Russian Orthodox Church, too, like so many other "followers" of Jesus, contributed to the campaign against Jewish people. Many Jews died in the pogroms at the hands of Russian soldiers called "Cossacks" in the early part of the twentieth century. Why were they killed? For one reason only: because they were Jews.

You may have seen the movie *Fiddler on the Roof*. Do you remember the violent raid that ruined the joy of the Jewish wedding celebration? And later, the orders given to the Jewish people to leave their little village and the only way of life they had ever known? Destruction and deportation were both common policies toward Jews in Czarist Russia. Many American Jews today are children or grandchildren of those who were beaten and expelled from Russia while the "Church" stood idly by. I'm one of them.

The Germany of World War II was mostly Catholic and Lutheran. In the writings of these "church fathers" and leaders of "Christianity," the Nazis found much justification for their atrocities.

I hesitate even to utter Jesus' name in the same sentence with the name Adolf Hitler, the one who ordered the torturous destruction of 6,000,000 Jews. Their teachings, after all, were diametrically opposed. Jesus taught love and compassion. Hitler taught hate. But I use the two together to make a point: Jewish people often confuse Christianity with the anti-Semitism of Nazism.

To illustrate this confusion let me share a personal story.

In 1975 my wife and I started an outreach in Skokie, a suburb of Chicago, to share the Good News with the many Jewish people living there. During that same period, a local neo-Nazi group planned a demonstration in Skokie, the home of many concentration camp survivors. You may remember *Skokie*, a made-for-TV movie, portraying the events and the conflict that ensued because of this demonstration.

Next door to our storefront office was a kosher butcher. My wife would often buy meat from him. We had developed a casual, pleasant relationship. During this time of tension in Skokie, I remember going into his shop, looking for an opportunity to talk about the Messiah. After awhile, when we were all alone, the butcher called me aside. I became excited thinking that perhaps we had gotten somewhere in our witness to him.

Rolling up his shirtsleeve, he pointed to a number tattooed across his forearm, the number he had received in a concentration camp in Poland during the Second World War. Then he whispered in a voice seething with bitterness and pain, "This is why I cannot believe in your Jesus!" He blindly confused Nazism with Christianity.

It was apparent that we had to do something for our people as the time for the Nazi march approached. We had to let them know that true Christianity and Nazi anti-Semitism were totally opposed beliefs.

I gathered together our small staff, a few volunteers, and some Christian friends and asked if they would join us in a demonstration in front of the Nazi headquarters on the south side of Chicago. Our purpose was to make a clear statement to the Jewish people that true Christians abhor Nazism. After much prayer, we set out to plan the demonstration. Although I, for one, usually shy away from this kind of risky confrontation, we all felt compelled to make a statement.

We created colorful placards bearing slogans like "Nazism is anti-Christian," "Jesus was not a Nazi," and "Jesus is the Messiah." Alerting both the media (in order to make the statement) and the police department (in order to protect us), we drove down to the Nazi headquarters and held an orderly, legal demonstration in front of their building.

Notifying the police had been a smart thing to do. Right in the middle of our demonstration, the Nazis dramatically threw open their heavy garage doors and stood menacingly in closed ranks, brandishing large guns across their chests. I could feel my heart pound as the sweat began to pour. But we kept praying and standing our ground.

TV cameras came to film the event, but the police quickly whisked us away to protect us. In fact, I and two or three of my lieutenants were taken away in a paddy wagon to reduce the tension. Ironically, the other person with us in the paddy wagon was the leader of the Nazi group, Frank Collin, whom I discovered later was a self-hating Jew, whose given last name was Cohen OY!

But our goal had been accomplished. Our statement was made. That evening, the media reported on the demonstration; articles were published that told our story. After that, many Jewish people living in Skokie came by our office to thank us for taking a public stand against the Nazis. Even the kosher butcher seemed friendlier.

Those of us in Jewish ministry are sometimes told that our motives are worse than those of Hitler. "The Nazis destroyed Jewish bodies, but *you* destroy Jewish souls," we are told. Jewish parents are often crushed when their children accept Yeshua. Spouses, too, go through their share of grief over a loved one who professes belief in the Messiah.

Naturally, to be misunderstood hurts. But we cannot deny the Messiahship of Yeshua even if it does hurt. We knew we couldn't erase the pain of those who had been through the concentration camps. But the eyes of many in Skokie saw that true believers would stand up against Nazism. Testimonies such as this one go a long way toward overcoming 2000 years of poor "Christian"-Jewish relations.

There are thousands of testimonies of true believers who stood with the Jews in Nazi Germany, risking and sometimes losing their lives to protect and hide them. Corrie ten Boom's *The Hiding Place* is a wonderful story of how a true Christian feels about the Jewish people. It's worth reading and even sharing with your Jewish neighbor.

You might be asking yourself why there is such confusion about this in the first place. Why should Jewish people make a connection between Christianity and Nazism?

To begin with, Adolf Hitler was born into a Catholic family. Since Jewish people are *born* Jewish, they automatically assume that Hitler was *born* Christian.

Furthermore, many in the Nazi party faithfully attended church. Observing the Nazis on the weekend, and then watching what they did during the week, many Jewish people raised the logical question, "If their church preached love, how could these church-going people practice hate?" The false conclusion they reached was that anti-Semitism was somehow part of Christian teaching. Unfortunately, sometimes it was true.

Granted, churches nowadays don't teach persecution of Jews, but I have sat in large evangelical churches and heard comments and remarks that revealed latent anti-Semitic attitudes. One time I heard a preacher lambaste "those self-righteous, hypocritical Pharisees!" He neglected to state that the unrighteous behavior he spoke of was possibly the exception, not the rule. He also forgot to mention those Pharisees who became followers of Jesus—Paul, Nicodemus, Joseph of Arimathea, and thousands more.

If you're going to be effective in your witness, you'll need to recognize the perceptions and misperceptions of your Jewish neighbor. As kind as you are, as honest and decent and neighborly as you have been, you must also understand that the memory of these unforgettable atrocities will be ever present in your neighbor's mind. Although you don't carry the sword of the Crusader, although you are not offering the ultimatum of the Inquisitor, although you do not spout the anti-Jewish diatribe of a Nazi, you are still identified as one of "them"—a non-Jew. A potential anti-Semite.

Jewish people often classify the world into "us" and "them." Jews have learned that, given the right degree of pressure, the right amount of propaganda, almost anyone is capable of persecuting a Jewish scapegoat. Jews have been warned by those who have lived through the Holocaust, "Remember, it *can* happen again!"

As a word of encouragement to you, know that you really can overcome "Church" history through an honest, open, loving friendship with your Jewish neighbor. But first, you need to understand how you, a Gentile believer, may be seen.

In the next chapter you will learn how to make yourself more credible to your Jewish neighbors so that you might be more effective in your witness. You can become more an "us," and less a "them."

— 4 —

HOW TO HAVE A MORE CREDIBLE WITNESS

— or —

Being a Little Jewish Wouldn't Hurt

Remember the old TV show *Dragnet*? When Joe Friday would question someone, he'd insist on "The facts, ma'am, just the facts."

We'd all like to believe we make our decisions based solely on the facts. But it's not true. If it were, car dealers wouldn't promote automobiles by using sexy women or handsome men. Politicians wouldn't spend millions on marketing to improve their images. Preachers wouldn't worry about their delivery; they'd just teach the words of Scripture.

Persuasion rarely occurs just because of facts. Often, what reaches us is a salesman's looks, a candidate's "charisma," or a preacher's presentation. Facts are sometimes secondary.

This ability to influence another is often called "credibility." We might hear two speakers saying precisely the same thing, but one will have greater impact on us than the other. If the scripts are the same, the difference in impact can be attributed to the speaker's credibility. Somehow we perceive him as more believable, more trustworthy, more reliable. In a word, more persuasive.

Credibility is sometimes viewed as a God-given gift. Either you're born with it or you're not. Social scientists who have studied credibility have drawn different conclusions. They say it can be attained. A person who is perceived as having greater credibility will bring about more attitude change and persuasion in a listener than one who is not. We know this is true!

How do certain teachers get more out of their students? What makes some bosses successful in motivating their employees? Why do certain pastors or rabbis achieve substantially greater impact on their congregations than others? If the content of the messages is basically the same—learn, work, or grow—to what can we attribute the difference in impact? The difference is credibility.

People have pondered this for centuries. Credibility was discussed as far back as Plato and Aristotle. In more recent years, experts in communication have delved into the study of credibility, emerging with some valuable insights.

In the late 1960s and early 1970s, I taught communications at Howard University in Washington, D.C. One of the most important topics in my class on persuasion was credibility. Even then, when credibility research was in its first few years, dozens of books and hundreds of articles had already been written on the subject.

I'll mention a few of the conclusions reached in credibility research in order to prepare you to be more persuasive communicating the Gospel to Jewish people.

Social scientists and communications experts reported that credibility is based primarily on four character traits: trustworthiness, expertness, identification, and dynamism. Each of these traits was identified and measured. Those having a high degree of each of these characteristics were usually more effective in persuading others. Now let's examine each characteristic.

Trustworthiness

Trustworthiness is the trait that encourages a person to feel safe with another. It is related to warmth, friendliness, and openness. A trustworthy person "doesn't have a mean bone in his body."

Dan Rigney is just such a person. I first met Dan at a special Hebrew-Christian *Rosh HaShanah* service. *Rosh HaShanah* is the Jewish New Year, the first of the High Holy Days. At the time we first met, Dan was a missionary with the American Board of Missions to the Jews, now known as Chosen People Ministries. I was not a believer, but I was curious about what a Hebrew-Christian service was. At the time I was engaged to a "Christian" woman and thought this kind of "compromise" service might be good for us. After all, I was a Hebrew (although Jews don't call themselves that), and she was a "Christian" (although I don't think she was "born again").

There was Dan, sporting a nice, long, rabbi-like beard and wearing white rabbinical robes and a miter, a white head covering. This garb is worn to remind the congregation of the priests' clothes in ancient Israel. But sticking out from under his robe was something I'd never seen a rabbi wear—cowboy boots!

During the service I heard many traditional Hebrew prayers. I also heard many Jewish people giving their testimonies. It didn't take me long to realize that this was not just a Jewish service that was open to Christians, or a congregation for interfaith marriages (my original assumption); this was a service where both Jews and Gentiles believed in Jesus as the Messiah and Savior.

After the service, I went up to Dan, and in a rather accusatory manner said, "You're no Jew! You're just pretending to be a Jew." The cowboy boots, coupled with his poor Hebrew pronunciations, were dead giveaways.

But his warm smile and honest words disarmed me. "No, I'm not Jewish, but I love the Jewish people because of Jesus. I'm a grafted-in Gentile."

I no longer felt combative. Dan's sincerity was so real it was tangible. Immediately, I found him to be safe, and therefore trustworthy and credible. I wanted to know more. I began attending Dan's weekly Bible study, where I later met the Messiah.

Trustworthiness is not something that can be trumped up. As we walk in the Messiah's light and become more like him, we grow toward being totally trustworthy. Growth and maturity naturally yield credibility. The fruits of the Spirit—love, joy, peace, patience, kindness, goodness, faithfulness, humility, and self-control (Galatians 5:22-23)—contribute toward making us trustworthy people, more credible *and* more persuasive.

(A word of caution: Some individuals buy the lie that no one should be involved in service for the Lord until he or she is perfect. They say, "I'm too big a sinner for anyone to listen to *me*!" Nothing could be further from the truth. Paul struggled with the flesh continually, but that didn't stop him from preaching. There is not a preacher, pastor, missionary, or Bible school teacher who is perfect. Yet all trust the Lord to enable them to fulfill God's calling for them. Don't allow your imperfection to be an excuse not to share the Good News.)

You are called to bring the Good News back to God's people, the Jews. Everyone could be more trustworthy, but God uses the imperfect, fallible sinner every day. The important thing to remember is to be honest in your testimony.

Life on this earth has its share of problems and pain. To act like nothing is wrong is to deny reality. That would be disingenuous, even in the interest of a testimony. The Lord blesses his people with a variety of growth experiences, including painful ones.

To deny what is obvious is misleading to those to whom we are witnessing. They are often more aware of our problems than we'd like to admit. It's all right to tell your Jewish friend about the problems you face. He or she may be able to help you. This will actually make you more trustworthy, since your Jewish friend deserves to know you as a person.

I was conducting a seminar on sharing the Messiah with Jewish people. One of the participants was experiencing tremendous personal suffering in her life. Divorce, death, depression. When we came to this section on trustworthiness and credibility she said she felt inadequate to share the Messiah. She decided to wait until all was well in her life. I felt that, to the contrary, it was just then that she should have shared.

Her Jewish friend would have related to her suffering and might have offered to help her. Admitting trouble would have made her real and would have shown her that to be a believer doesn't mean you have to have it all together.

Also, she could have been a Job-like testimony. Job, in the midst of his severe suffering, affirmed his faith in God and the Messiah, and said, "But I know that my Redeemer lives, that in the end he will rise on the dust" (Job 19:25). Her Jewish friend would have been impressed with her trust in God.

Trustworthiness is an important factor in credibility and credibility is important to good communication and persuasion. God is molding his people into the image of the trustworthy savior to make them more credible and persuasive in their witness.

Expertness

This is the area in which most well-meaning believers give up. I've heard things like, "How can I talk about the Bible to the people to whom this book was first given?" or, "I'd love to witness to my Jewish neighbor, but he's too smart for me."

It's true that Jewish people were the ones chosen by God to first receive his holy Word. It is also true that Jewish people highly prize a good education. But surprisingly, today Jewish people are relatively illiterate when it comes to the Bible, and I don't mean just the New Testament. Most Jews, the vast majority, have never read the *Old* Testament.

Even those Jewish people who go to synagogue regularly read only certain parts of Scripture. You see, on each Sabbath day only a portion of Scripture is read—something from the *Torah* (Genesis through Deuteronomy) and something from the Prophets or Writings. A Jewish person who has done his Bible reading in synagogue every Saturday still will not have read the entire Old Testament in the course of a year.

What's more incredible, much of the prophetic writing is completely ignored in the synagogues, especially those portions known as Messianic prophecies (to be discussed in Chapter 6). The average believer who has gone to church and attended Sunday school is better versed in the Hebrew Scriptures than his Jewish friend. You, relatively speaking, *are* the expert.

Even if you are confronted with a question you are not prepared to answer, be honest. I would prefer that a doctor tell me he needed to study or confer with a colleague about my symptoms than fake a diagnosis. Don't be afraid to admit, "I don't know, but I'll look it up and get back to you."

The words of the apostle Peter aptly conclude the subject of expertness. He admonished believers to be "always ready to give a reasoned answer to anyone who asks you to explain the hope you have in you—yet with humility and fear" (1 Peter 3:15). This was Peter's way of saying we should increase our expertness, tempering it with trustworthiness, so that we can become more credible witnesses. We are to be witnesses to *everyone*, including our Jewish neighbors.

Identification

It meant a lot to me that Dan Rigney had taken the trouble to identify with my people by wearing the rabbi's robes and speaking Hebrew. Though I was surprised and perhaps somewhat offended at first, his efforts triggered my curiosity. Then, when I sensed his genuine love for the Jewish people, I was glad he had chosen to make the identification. He desired, as much as possible, to become one of "us."

Likewise, when I've met Christians who enjoy Jewish culture, humor, or literature, it has always made me feel closer to them. Identification is a key ingredient of credibility.

Paul, apostle to the Gentiles, said, "with Jews, what I did was put myself in the position of a Jew, in order to win Jews." (1 Corinthians 9:20). Paul was, of course, already Jewish, but he emphasized this Jewishness to identify with the Jewish people. He was willing to submit to the traditions of his people. Furthermore, he was willing to take a Nazirite vow (Acts 18:18), something only a religious Jew would do. He followed the *Torah*. He summarized his religious life when addressing King Agrippa: "I have followed the strictest party in our religion" (Acts 26:5). He didn't do this for show; he was a sincere Pharisee. But there is a message here, too. If you want to win your Jewish friend to the Messiah, it helps to understand his frame of mind—to become more like him—to appreciate the things he regards as special, significant, even sacred. Paul's life demonstrated that.

Identifying with someone increases credibility and persuasiveness. We are drawn to the political candidate who speaks for us and seems to understand our needs. We relate to the salesman who makes an effort to understand our wants. We even respond to the TV commercial that shows people whose lifestyles mirror our own.

In witnessing to Jewish people, it is indeed possible for a Gentile to identify. In Section III, I'll be discussing some of the characteristics of Jewish people, in generalities, of course. But here, let me say that if you want to be more credible in your witness, become an "us."

Learn what issues concern Jewish people most. Subscribe to the *Jerusalem Post* or your local Jewish newspaper. Attend lectures or celebrations sponsored by the local Jewish community. If you can, take a tour to Israel. In short, learn about the Jewish people.

Experience and enjoy the rich culture of God's chosen people. Understanding Jewish humor is a fun way to get started. Books such as *The Joys of Yiddish* and *A Treasury of Jewish Humor* are enjoyable and will help you get a feeling for the humor of Jewish people. You may even learn some new jokes. Of course, some of the current TV programs and movies give you a taste of Jewish humor — Mel Brooks, Woody Allen, Jerry Seinfeld, etc.

Jewish music can be fun, worshipful, and soul-stirring. You already hear strains of it hidden within the melodies of Barry Manilow, Paul Simon, Marvin Hamlisch, Kenny G. and others. But it's much more. You might enjoy going to a concert of Jewish music with your Jewish neighbor.

Literature is terribly important to God's chosen people. Books by Chaim Potok—for example, *The Chosen* and *My Name is Asher Lev*—offer keen insight into the New York Orthodox Jewish community, a community that has impacted Jews everywhere. Other writers such as Isaac Bashevis Singer and Sholom Aleichem will teach you about Jewish backgrounds and traditions. Herman Wouk is another important Jewish author, as is Leon Uris.

Gastronomics is also part of the Jewish life. You might already enjoy bagels. As I wrote in the preface to the second edition, since I first wrote this book, bagels have lost their strictly Jewish identity. Now you can buy a bagel at the supermarket, in some fast-food restaurants, and just about everywhere. Bagels have caught on.

In the 1960s, bagels were still viewed exclusively as a "Jewish" food. Since I considered them a necessary staple in my diet, I would always bring a few dozen bagels back to college after going home for the holidays. Ohio University in Athens, Ohio, didn't know about these odd-looking doughnut-shaped rolls. It wasn't long before I'd acquired the nickname "Bagels." My friends at college learned to love bagels.

One of my fraternity brothers accompanied me home during a vacation. To the honored guest, my mother served lox for breakfast, along with the bagels. Lox—smoked salmon—is a little like sushi, the Japanese raw fish delicacy. Somehow, my Midwestern friend couldn't get into it.

If you really want to identify with Jews, though, try some lox—but right after payday. A steady diet of it could put a dent in your budget! It's expensive and therefore eaten infrequently. However, just as bagels have made it into mainstream American gastronomic life, lox is now available in places other than a Jewish deli. My family buys lox at one of the popular warehouse-type supermarkets. It's less expensive than it used to be.

Eating lox will help you identify, and give you a real taste treat. But don't forget to put a *schmear* of cream cheese on the bagel before you add the lox.

Missionaries in foreign cultures have finally understood the message of identification. The traditional missionary approach had been to try to get those whom they sought to reach to become just like the folks back home. It became a goal to persuade the tribal native to succumb to the Western custom of wearing a tie. It wasn't just the Gospel the missionaries brought; it was Western culture.

But in recent years, missionaries have become sensitive to and appreciative of the culture of the people they seek to reach. Learning the native language and customs, today's missionaries encourage the development of indigenous churches. This practice is sometimes called cross-cultural communication; missiologists refer to it as contextualization, putting the Gospel into the context of the people with whom they are working. Identification helps persuasion.

Dynamism

The final trait that makes someone credible is dynamism, enthusiams for the message. I'm sure you've heard the TV sales pitches for used cars, weight-loss programs, or hair regrowth products. Marketing experts have discovered that a person who communicates with energy is going to be more effective than someone who speaks in a monotone.This has been proven by communication research.

If we're going to be credible, thus persuasive in our witness, we need to demonstrate dynamism.Yes, this mus be tempered by common sense, but it's an essential aspect of credibility. And aren't Yeshua and his message something to get excited about!

Trustworthiness, expertness, identification, and dynamism are the four foundation blocks upon which credibility is built.And remember, increased credibility generally leads to more effective communication and persuasion. Your mission, should you decide to accept it, is to grow in these four areas for your own personal enrichment as well as for the sake of your witness. Remember, yours is not a mission impossible.

Here in Section I, you've learned some of the reasons for bringing the Gospel to Jewish people and have been challenged to fulfill "the Gentile Great Commission"—provoke them to jealousy! You've learned the background of the "us/them" syndrome and the tragedies of "Christian"-Jewish history, both of which affect the way believers are perceived when they witness. And you've learned how to be more credible in your witness.

In the next section, the "Jewish Gospel," we will look at ways to present the Messiah that are both understandable and acceptable to Jewish people. It is critical not only to understand who you are and how you are perceived, but also that you learn to communicate in a Jewish way. That's what we'll look at next.

SECTION II

Your Message: The Jewish Gospel

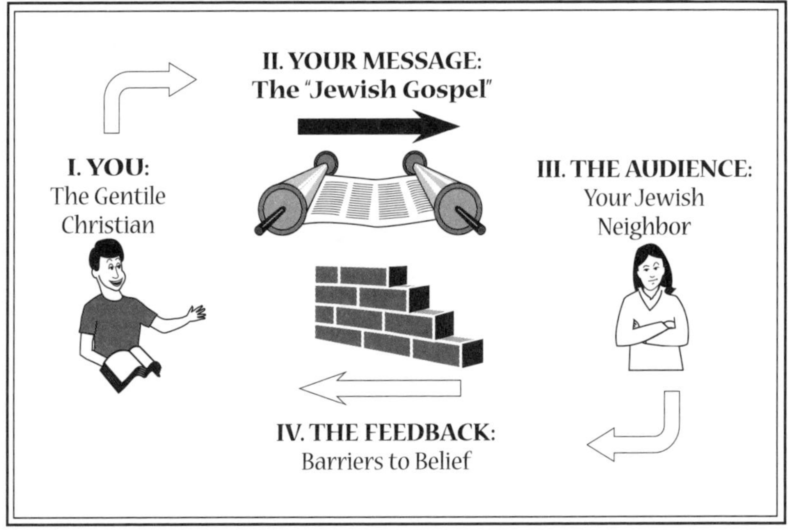

Back to our witnessing model. With increased comprehension about your role in Jewish evangelism gleaned from Section I, we can now focus our discussion on the message, namely, the "Jewish Gospel."

You might be thinking, "I thought there was only one Gospel. What's all this about a "Jewish Gospel?" Good question!

There is only one Gospel, just as there is only "one body and one Spirit . . . one Lord, one trust, one immersion, and one God, the Father of all" (Ephesians 4:4–6). But in this same passage, Paul explains that there is a variety of gifts in ministering the Gospel—emissaries, prophets, evangelists, proclaimers of the Good News, and shepherds and teachers (Ephesians 4:11). Likewise, there is a variety of approaches in communicating the message of the Messiah.

This is shown in the effective work done by campus outreaches. InterVarsity, Campus Crusade, Navigators, and others have a particular approach to working with college students. They minister a unique "college student" Gospel. Sometimes, churches are planted near campuses in order to minister specifically to the needs of college students. I saw this ministry in action when I spoke in just such a church planted next to a well-known southern California college.

Whereas most pastors tend to dress rather conservatively—dark suits, ties, wing tip shoes—the pastors of this church wore sport shirts, penny loafers, and Levis. The music in this campus church was played on guitar and had a contemporary sound, quite different from traditional church hymns played on piano or organ.

And unlike many church buildings, architecturally designed to inspire worship and induce awe, this church met in a cozy carpeted room where some sat on folding chairs and others on the floor.

I learned from this very successful campus church that college students can best be reached within their own cultural context. Comfortably cross-legged on that carpet, those young adults were more likely to listen to the Gospel than if they were sitting stiffly in a wooden pew.

The same principle holds true in witnessing to Jewish people. I suppose if those campus pastors were writing a book to help others reach out on the local campus, they might have entitled this section the "Campus Gospel," hoping to alert the reader to approach college students in a unique and more effective way.

That's why I call this section, the "Jewish Gospel." Not that Jewish people are saved in a different way from Gentiles, but that the Good News ought to be presented in a fashion that makes it easily understood by Jewish people. Remember, the Church has not always approached the people of Israel in a positive, loving way. It's time to try something different, something that just might work—the "Jewish Gospel."

— 5 —

THE GOOD NEWS IN THE OLD TESTAMENT

— or —

The "Jewish Gospel" in the "Jewish Bible"

Because I was preparing to become a teacher of Transcendental Meditation, I set out to devour as much of the teaching of the Maharishi as I could. A one-month teacher-training course in northern California fit right into my plans, and the plans of 1,400 other "seekers of truth." After this first month of training, I made plans to go to Majorca, Spain, for the second and third months to complete the course. God, however, had other plans for me.

Leaving California and returning home to Washington, D.C., I enrolled in a weekend T.M. retreat in the beautiful mountains of Virginia. The retreat included eight, nine and ten daily meditation sessions instead of the usual two. I was expecting to break through to "god-consciousness." But something else broke through, instead.

While deep in one of my meditations, I experienced "astral projection," also called "soul travel." I sensed that my soul was rising from my body, hovering near the ceiling, looking down upon my body sitting on the bed. It felt just as strange as it sounds! I was terrified! I had never before experienced such a supernatural event.

This bizarre experience was unsettling, so I looked around the room for something to read, to take my mind off what had just happened. I couldn't find anything other than T.M. pamphlets, T.M. booklets, and other T.M. materials. And a Gideon-placed Bible.

"This will be a nice change of pace," I thought, as I opened the book. Jewish Bibles and prayer books open from what you might call the back. Hebrew reads from right to left. So I turned to the "back" of the Bible, figuring I'd open to Genesis and read about the beginning of the world. Instead, I found myself in the midst of something mysterious. It was called "The Revelation to John," an unusual place to begin reading the Bible!

When I realized that I was in the New Testament, an uneasiness swept over me. This was the book, or so I had been taught, that spoke about the Gentile god, Jesus. It had nothing to do with Jews. We Jews were taught to stay away from this "dangerous" document. In fact, a Jewish tradition held that a Jew who holds a New Testament will see his hands rot!

The rabbis gave this warning to their people to keep them from being seduced into following Jesus, the one they held accountable for all the anti-Semitic acts throughout history. This fear was so deep that I was not even permitted to utter the name of Jesus in my home.

I wanted to avoid the New Testament at all costs. It was the Bible for the Gentiles. I didn't want to violate some ancient Jewish law that maybe I didn't know about. (That's why I use and promote the *Complete Jewish Bible*, a version that restores the original Jewishness to the entire bible. Because of centuries of latent —and not so latent—anti-Semitism among translators, most New Testaments feel like books written by Gentiles. The *Comlete Jewish Bible* feels Jewish and is enjoyed by believers wishing to recapture the Jewish roots of their faith.)

As I innocently turned to the Revelation, a verse caught my eye: one hundred and forty-four thousand Jewish believers in Jesus saying "Victory to our God, who sits on the throne, and to the Lamb" (7:10).

After getting over the shock that I was in the New Testament, and after seeing that nothing bad had happened to me, I laughed, "Ha! Jews who follow Jesus. I'll believe that when I see it! Jews don't believe in Jesus." Vindicated by my declaration, I tossed that Bible across the room. I felt the subject was closed. (Don't worry, I've had many opportunities to apologize to and thank the Gideons for their ministry since becoming a believer!)

Most Jews consider the New Testament irrelevant at best and blasphemous at worst. Although it's possible to lead a Jew to the Messiah by quoting exclusively from the New Testament, it is wiser to begin with what is already familiar, or at least accepted as Jewish, that is, the Old Testament, or *Tanakh.*

In this chapter, then, I will outline some premises from the *Tanakh* that you can share with your Jewish neighbor once you have established yourself as a credible friend.

Premise 1: God Loves the Jewish People

We're all familiar with the carrot-or-stick approach to motivation—reward or punishment. Sometimes both are necessary to get a mule to move, but it certainly seems more humane to try the carrot before resorting to the stick.The same holds true when dealing with people.

A boss can motivate his employees to produce quality work through threats and punishment,but the inducement of reward is more inspiring.A teacher can lambaste his students into learning, but in the long run,positive reinforcement is more successful.A parent can harass his or her children into obedience and submission, but loving them into the proper relationship promotes better behavior.

When witnessing to the truth of Messiah Yeshua, love will go a lot farther than fear. It is true that fear can motivate, but it also promotes a relationship fraught with mistrust and anxiety. On top of this, Jewish people already struggle with a rather generalized guilt.

No one knows exactly where this guilt comes from. Perhaps from a deep awareness of failing to keep God's Law. Maybe from millennia of rejection by the rest of the world.Whatever the source, this guilt is a real component of the Jewish psyche today.

The first step, then, in presenting the Gospel in the Old Testament is to let Jewish people know that God indeed loves them. My favorite verse to communicate this truth with is,

> *Adonai* didn't set his heart on you or choose you because you numbered more than any other people—on the contrary, you were the fewest of all peoples. Rather, it was because *Adonai* loved you, and because he wanted to keep the oath which he had sworn to your ancestors ... Deuteronomy 7:7-8

There's a cost to being chosen. Sometimes it has an expensive price tag. But Jews have learned at least to have a sense of humor about it.

In *Fiddler on the Roof*, an enjoyable movie and play that gives an inside look at life in the "old" country, Tevye, the papa, takes stock of his life. He has five unmarried daughters, a dry milk cow, a lame horse, plenty of poverty, and to top it off, a more-than-occasional attack from his neighbors, the Cossacks.

Considering his situation, Tevye raises his eyes and looks to heaven. "I know we're the chosen people, but once in a while can't you choose someone else for a change?"

Nearly all Jews have felt like this at one time or another. It's hard to reconcile the reality of the Holocaust with a loving God who chose us. We'll deal with that question later, but in spite of all the pain, it's necessary for your Jewish neighbor to know that God uniquely chose and especially loves the Jewish people.

Premise 2: Sin Has Broken the Love Relationship Between God and Israel

"O.K., O.K.," your Jewish neighbor relents, "God chose me and loves me. So kindly explain all the suffering the Jewish people have had to endure. And what about *my* problems, while you're at it?"

Today, most Jewish people—most people, for that matter—have done their best to ignore the question of sin. Psychologists use terms like *aberrant conduct* or *socially unacceptable behavior*. Some groups, like the T.M. people, blame stress and strain. Others avoid the subject of sin by promoting the relativism of morality. Many have abandoned traditional moral values, and replaced them with new ideas.

A Bible believer knows that *sin* is the source of humankind's problems and that there is a need to return to the biblical explanation of man's bad behavior. The prophet Isaiah recognized sin to be the problem in Israel's relationship to God:

> It is your own crimes that separate you from your God; your sins have hidden his face from you, so that he doesn't hear.
> Isaiah 59:2

Without a relationship with God, one cannot experience peace and fulfillment. Because of sin, Israel in general and your Jewish neighbor in particular experience broken relationships with a loving God. But in his mercy, God has made provision.

Premise 3: God's Solution to the Sin Problem is Messiah's Sacrifice

In the Garden of Eden, or as Jewish people say, *Gan Eden*, Adam and Eve sinned. Previous to their sin, the Lord God had said,

> You may freely eat from every tree in the garden except the tree of the knowledge of good and evil. You are not to eat from it, because on the day that you eat from it, it will become certain that you will die. Genesis 2:16–17

Here, at the beginning of human history, God made it plain that it was essential that his people heed his Word. Humankind, however, failed to listen. Sin exacted a price; that price had to be paid. But God had anticipated that failure and provided a system of substitutionary atonement to cover the penalty for human sin.

In the Garden of Eden, an animal provided "garments of skin for Adam and his wife" after they sinned (Genesis 3:21). The animal's skin covered their shame. A substitutionary death was needed.

Later, in the *Torah*, God provided an elaborate sacrificial system for his people Israel, anticipating their failure to obey the Mosaic Law. Again, blood was to be shed for the sins of his people:

> For the life of a creature is in the blood, and I have given it to you on the altar to make atonement for yourselves . . .
> Leviticus 17:11

In his infinite wisdom, God realized that his people would not live up to his standards for them. But in his infinite mercy, he made provision for his people's sins through substitutionary, or vicarious, atonement. This is an example of the "life for a life" principle. Because of sin, something had to die.

God repeatedly provided atonement. Yet the final provision for the sin of Israel and for the world would entail a more costly, more dramatic display of love. This is what "Jesus died for our sins" means. He provided atonement—at-one-ment—a restored relationship with God. His death is the provision for sin.

These three premises provide the basis for presenting the Gospel to your Jewish neighbor from the Old Testament.

Premise 1	God loves the Jewish people
Premise 2	Sin has broken the relationship between God and Israel.
Premise 3	God's solution to the sin problem is Messiah's sacrifice.

All you need to do now is to show how Yeshua became the ultimate sacrifice offered by God to provide atonement, reconciliation, and restoration between God and his people, Israel. For this, we need to look at the subject known as Messianic prophecy.

— 6 —

MESSIANIC PROPHECY

— or —

"It says that in my Bible?"

People love prophecy! Tabloids flank the supermarket checkout lines announcing the predictions of men and women who claim to have the gift of prophecy. A new Christian book appears every month, or so it seems, with the latest on the future. Whether these forecasts turn out to be right or wrong, readers are still drawn to them and remain titillated by the possibility of supernatural foreknowledge.

In the Bible, God used prophecy to admonish his people about their present sinful behavior and warn them of the consequences. At times, prophecy foretold the future usually in connection with these warnings. Other times it was a message of hope focusing on the coming Messiah.

Could there have been any information more significant for the Israelites than the details of the one yet to come, the one who would rescue Israel from an often desperate situation? Nothing captured the imagination and longing of the Jews more powerfully than the hope of the coming Messiah.

God presented his people with a portrait of the Anointed One, the Messiah. This portrait was painted in the brushstrokes of what we call Messianic prophecy—predictions about the coming Messiah.

I saw a book once that claimed to have discovered as many as 333 Messianic prophecies in the Old Testament. Those who offer Messianic prophecy when witnessing to Jewish people, however, don't usually deal with more than a dozen selections of Scripture. This chapter will highlight the most effective and most commonly used Messianic prophecies so that you may better understand how to incorporate these portions of Scripture when sharing with your Jewish neighbor.

When I conduct seminars for churches and groups, I'm asked many of the same questions. One that invariably crops up is, "If these Messianic prophecies are so clear, why don't the Jewish people believe them and recognize their Messiah?" The answer may surprise you.

Most Jewish people have never seen Messianic prophecies!

"How can this be," I'm asked, "when they're right there in the Old Testament?" While it is true that the prophecies that point to Jesus/Yeshua can be found in the *Tanakh*, it is also true, as I said before, that most Jews have never read the Old Testament.

In the past, rabbis, in their desire to protect their people from straying, would prohibit the reading of Christian literature. Due to the tremendous persecution against Jews in the name of Jesus, the leaders of the Jewish people didn't want their flocks to be seduced by what *appeared* to be an anti-Jewish religion. To ensure loyalty and to prevent curiosity, Messianic prophecies were deliberately eliminated from the traditional weekly Bible readings.

One can appreciate the intentions of the rabbis. Considering their wish to hold their people together, this protective approach is understandable. They were using the limited light they had. Unfortunately, this approach denied the full Word of God to the people of Israel, much the same way Catholics were kept from reading the Bible for many centuries.

Messianic prophecy is something with which few Jews are familiar. Furthermore, since the doctrine of the Messiah has fallen from prominence in Judaism, mention of Messianic prophecy is omitted from most Jewish religious schools. Ninety-nine percent of Jewish people have *never* heard the expression, "Messianic prophecy." It's usually a Christian who brings up the issue of Messianic prophecy.

The fact is, however, that Messianic prophecy was given by God so that his people might know about the coming Messiah, that they would await the arrival of their king, and that they would recognize him at his birth.

Prophecy is part of God's Word and can accomplish the purposes for which it was given, namely, to point Jewish people to Yeshua, the Messiah.

It's good to know, also, that it's not just Christians who considered these portions of Scripture to be Messianic and predictive in nature. They were considered Messianic by the rabbis of old. This information is compiled and available in books, both from Jewish and Christian writers.

The writings of the rabbis often refer to these very same prophecies as Messianic. But only observant Jews, a small part of the Jewish population, read these writings. "Christian" anti-Semitism has persuaded Jewish scholars to attribute other interpretations to many of these Messianic passages.

True believers in Yeshua can break through the walls built up because of the horrendous history of Church/synagogue relations. With love, armed with Messianic prophecies, it can be done.

Establish the Role of the Prophet

Abraham, Isaac, Jacob, Moses—these are some of the biblical names with which the Jewish community is comfortable. But Haggai, Zephaniah, Amos, and Micah are not so familiar. Jewish people don't think much about the prophets of Israel and rarely read what they had to say.

When prophets are discussed, they are usually seen in the role of social reformers. But the prophets of ancient Israel performed another important role, as stated earlier. Their prophecies often pointed to the Messiah. These men were chosen not just to call the people of Israel back to God; they were selected to predict some very important future events.

The Lord created the office of prophet and gave the job description in the *Torah*:

> I will raise up for them a prophet like you from among their kinsmen. I will put my words in his mouth, and he will tell them everything I order him. Whoever doesn't listen to my words, which he will speak in my name, will have to account for himself to me. Deuteronomy 18:18–19

The office of prophet was established because the children of Israel could not bear to hear the voice of God directly. God understood this and accommodated them, but the accommodation had some rules.

If a person spoke in the name of God, but was not really a prophet, he was to die:

> But if a prophet presumptuously speaks a word in my name which I didn't order him to say, or if he speaks in the name of other gods, then that prophet must die.
>
> Deuteronomy 18:20

The test for authenticity hinged upon the accuracy of the prediction:

> When a prophet speaks in the name of *Adonai*, and the prediction does not come true—that is, the word is not fulfilled—then *Adonai* did not speak that word. The prophet who said it spoke presumptuously; you have nothing to fear from him. Deuteronomy 18:22

True prophets foretold future events because God wanted his people to know about them. For Israel, nothing was more important than the coming Messiah. Who would he be? How would he come? Where would he be born? When would he arrive? Finally, what would he do?

Some Useful Messianic Prophecies

The Suffering Servant, Isaiah 53

Without question, the Messianic prophecy that has had the greatest impact on Jewish people has been Isaiah 53. I remember vividly the day I was first shown the portrait of the sinless suffering servant of God.

I had been attending a Bible study conducted by Dan Rigney, the missionary with the cowboy boots. Dan was now teaching from the book of Isaiah. The first chapter mentions sin and cleansing:

> Even if your sins are like scarlet, they will be white as snow;
> even if they are red as crimson, they will be like wool.
>
> Isaiah 1:18

"What sins?!" I challenged. Espousing the teachings of T.M., I continued. "My problems aren't caused by sin; they're caused by stress and strain."

I was ignorant about sin; remember, it's not a hot topic for rabbinic sermons, so I hadn't heard much about it. But I had begun to feel more convinced about sin in my life, even though I didn't knowingly accept the standards of God's Law. The Word of God was having its way on my heart.

One night at the Bible study, Dan opened his Bible and asked us to turn to Isaiah 53. There, right before me, was a vivid description of someone who gave his life to atone for the sins of his people. Following the lesson, Dan asked me for my comments. "That was nice," I remarked coolly, "and I'd love to believe it, but you've obviously taken some New Testament portion and stuck it in the Old Testament. Anyone can see that those verses are talking about Jesus!" I felt tricked.

I turned to the front of the Bible and pointed to where it indicated that he had been reading from the King James Version of Scripture. Definitely, this was not a Jewish version.

"I'll have to check out those verses in my own *Jewish* Bible," I argued. But where was my Bible? I hadn't seen it since the day of my *Bar Mitzvah*, when I stopped observing many of the practices of Judaism.

I drove over to my parents' home, trotted down the steps to the recreation room, and found my old Bible on top of the bookshelf. Reaching up, I removed it, blew off the dust, and hunted for Isaiah 53. There, to my shock, I found the very same words I had read in the "Christian" Bible. I felt as if a bolt of lightning were shooting through me as I realized Jesus/Yeshua was the one of whom Isaiah had spoken.

My parents and their friends were upstairs playing bridge. Taking the steps two at a time, I waved my open Bible and cried, "I've found the Messiah!" Strange, I thought, no one seemed to appreciate the significance of my discovery. In fact, from the look on everyone's face, I think I may have ruined their evening.

But I was now convinced that Yeshua was the Messiah. Isaiah 53 got to me.

When you read the Scripture's description of the suffering servant, you see a man going quietly to his death in order to pay for the sins of his people. You watch a man die with criminals, yet get buried with the rich. You learn about one who would be sinless, yet bear the sins of many, performing an intercessory role. You discover that the Lord was pleased to sacrifice this person as a guilt offering—one who would see his seed after his death. It is a picture of the life, death, and resurrection of the Messiah.

In ancient times, the rabbis taught that this portion of Scripture spoke of the Messiah. In order to reconcile a Messiah who would die and then reign as king, they offered a two-Messiah theory to explain the dual role the Messiah would have. *Mashiach* Ben-Yosef (Messiah Son of Joseph) and *Mashiach* Ben-David (Messiah Son of David) were the names given to these "two" Messiahs.

The first, in the likeness of Joseph, Jacob's beloved son who was sold into slavery by his jealous brothers, would bear the sins of his people. The second, in the spirit of King David, would reign over Israel. Isaiah 53 was the portion used to explain the sacrificial role of the Messiah. And, as we will see in a moment, the prophet Zechariah foretold his rule as king.

Isaiah 53 does not require a great deal of interpretation. The portrait is painted clearly enough for those with eyes to see:

> People despised and avoided him, a man of pains, well acquainted with illness. Like someone from whom people turn their faces, he was despised; we did not value him. In fact, it was our diseases he bore, our pains from which he suffered; yet we regarded him as punished, stricken and afflicted by God. But he was wounded because of our crimes,

> crushed because of our sins; the disciplining that makes us whole fell on him, and by his bruises we are healed. We all, like sheep, went astray; we turned, each one, to his own way; yet *Adonai* laid on him the guilt of all of us. . . . Therefore I will assign him a share with the great, he will divide the spoil with the mighty, for having exposed himself to death and being counted among the sinners, while actually bearing the sin of many and interceding for the offenders. Isaiah 53:3–6, 12

The present-day rabbinic interpretation of this passage is that it describes Israel, not the Messiah. This interpretation was first suggested around 1100 C.E. by Rashi, the great rabbi. At that time, there was severe persecution of Jews by "Christians." These "Christians" held that Isaiah 53 pertained to Messiah. Therefore, Rashi interpreted this passage so it was no longer considered Messianic, lest some of his people "mistakenly" end up following the "enemy." By the 1500s, a non-Messianic interpretation had been established.

It is true that Jewish people have suffered greater atrocities than perhaps any other single group on the face of the earth; nevertheless, Isaiah 53 is clearly not talking about Israel. It can't be. Try substituting Israel each time the prophet speaks of the "servant" or "he" or "him." It simply won't work. The plain sense of the text does not support the modern Jewish interpretation of the passage. It has to be talking about a person.

When Philip (the evangelist) was traveling from Jerusalem to Gaza along an old desert road, he met an Ethiopian eunuch, most likely a proselyte to Judaism (Acts 8:26–40).

The eunuch "had been to Yerushalayim [Jerusalem] to worship" and was sitting in his carriage, reading the prophet Isaiah. God told Philip, "Go over to this chariot . . ." The eunuch was reading Isaiah 53. Puzzled, he said to Philip, a Jewish believer in Messiah, "Here's my question to you—is the prophet talking about himself or someone else?" (Acts 8:34)

Philip got a chance to share about Yeshua with his "neighbor." The eunuch was so excited to find the Messiah that he showed his commitment by immediately getting immersed.

Recently I shared Isaiah 53 with a member of my family. I didn't reveal to whom I thought it referred. After reading the portion, my Jewish relative said, "But this doesn't say the Jews killed Jesus, does it?" She knew it referred to Messiah's death. She was struggling with the anti-Semitic lie that the Jews killed the Messiah.

When I told her it certainly did not say that the Jews killed Jesus, but instead indicated that God was pleased with the sacrifice of the suffering servant, she felt better. Imagine her surprise when I pointed out that it had been written 700 years before Messiah was born. Before we departed she asked, "Where was that portion of Scripture, again?"

Without a doubt, Isaiah 53 is the most compelling of all the Messianic prophecies, describing the mission of the coming Messiah. Isaiah is not the only prophet to describe the work of the Messiah. While he does give the clearest account of the substitutionary role—that of "Messiah Son of Joseph"—the role of the reigning King, "Messiah Son of David" is vividly presented to us by the prophet Zechariah.

The Conquering King, Zechariah 12–14

Never before in the history of the world has the prophecy of Zechariah been more timely. Today we find Israel gathered in her own land, surrounded by hostile nations, outnumbered 100 to 1, unpopular with much of the rest of the world. One can almost see Zechariah's prophecy coming to pass, as if we were "in that day."

The setting for the prophecy is a day of danger for Israel. The beginnings of both chapter 12 and chapter 14 describe a time of enormous peril, with all the nations of the world gathered together to destroy Jerusalem. But in that day, God promised to save his people.

The Lord warns that anyone who attacks Jerusalem will be severely hurt, for she will be a heavy stone to lift. Imagine the strain felt by a man who attempts to lift a weight heavier than he is able to bear. You can hear the anguish and see the grimace etched upon his face. You can feel the muscles of his back strain to the limit as the burden proves to be too much. Picturing this, we can understand the pain the hostile nations will suffer as they try in vain to budge God's fortress, Jersualem.

Then, when the attack against Israel is at its worst, and it is apparent that no other nations can or will help her, Israel will call upon God for help. He will then pour out his Spirit upon the house of David and the inhabitants of Jerusalem, giving "a spirit of grace and prayer." This outpouring will cause the Jewish people to "look to me, whom they pierced. They will mourn for him as one mourns for an only son" (Zechariah 12:10). No one can recognize the truth of the Messiah unless it is revealed by the Spirit of God. Here, "in that day," when the Spirit is poured out, all of Israel will have open eyes, eyes to know the Messiah.

In that day, when all the nations gather themselves against Jerusalem, God himself will go forth and fight on behalf of his people. His feet will stand on the Mount of Olives (Zechariah 14:3) and he will rebuff those who have dared to attack God's chosen people. The Mount of Olives is the site where Messiah wept over Jerusalem, lamenting the suffering his people would undergo because of their refusal to trust him (Matthew 23:37). It is the place from which he ascended into heaven (Luke 24:50). It is also the place where he will return (Zechariah 14:4).

Zechariah 13:1 promises, "a spring will be opened up for the house of David and the people living in Yerushalayim to cleanse them from sin and impurity." In that day, cleansing for Israel will be found in the sacrifice of the Messiah.

In that day, living water will flow from Jerusalem (Zechariah 14:8). The promise of spiritual life will issue from the heart of God. Yeshua, talking to the woman at the well, informed her that he was the source of that living water (John 4:14).

Finally, those nations that remain following the attack on Israel (these will be individuals who have sided with God) will go up to Jerusalem year after year to worship the king, the Lord of hosts. Complete now will be the Messiah's final mission; accomplished will be his ultimate goal—to reign as king over all the earth.

These prophecies in Zechariah have not yet been fulfilled. All the nations of the world have not yet turned against Israel. The

Spirit has not yet been poured out upon the Jewish people. The Messiah has not yet returned to the Mount of Olives.

Thus, the two roles of the Messiah are clearly seen in these two Messianic prophecies. The first, that of suffering servant—Messiah Son of Joseph—is depicted in Isaiah 53. The second role, that of conquering king—Messiah Son of David—is described in Zechariah 12-14. These two powerful passages of Messianic prophecy can persuade Jewish people that Yeshua (Jesus) is the Messiah. And there are many more that support this conclusion.

The Entering King, Zechariah 9:9

Zechariah 9:9 tells us by what means of transportation the Messiah would come to Jerusalem. He would ride on a young donkey. This paints a curious picture. One might think the Messiah would enter the city where he would one day reign on different transportation.

Ordinarily, a king would enter a city sitting grandly astride a war horse, both horse and rider armored for battle. This exhibit of strength and power was designed to intimidate his foes. We see this done today when nations participate in military exercises to show others their might.

The Messiah would come on a young donkey because his was a mission of peace, not conquest. Matthew 21:2-6 describes the fulfillment of this prophecy as Messiah rode into Jerusalem on a donkey in "triumphal entry." His was a display of meekness, not of might.

The Everlasting King, 2 Samuel 7:12-17

This portion of Scripture accomplishes two things at once. It prophesies that a son of King David would reign over Israel and that the Kingdom under David's rule would endure forever.

David's life was drawing to its close. God had sent Nathan the prophet to the king to offer him a promise of hope in his declining years. Speaking of Solomon, Nathan said:

> When your days come to an end and you sleep with your ancestors, I will establish one of your descendants to succeed you, one of your own flesh and blood; and I will set up his rulership. He will build a house for my name, and I will establish his royal throne forever. 2 Samuel 7:12-13

Solomon did indeed "build a house for [God's] name," but Solomon did not live or rule forever. How, then, was the throne of his kingdom to continue eternally, especially given the fact that Solomon's Temple was eventually destroyed and that Israel no longer crowns kings? The answer is through the Messiah. This son, this descendant of David, would ultimately establish an everlasting kingdom.

The genealogies of Messiah show that he was, in fact, a descendant of David. The first chapter of Matthew traces his heritage from Abraham, to David, to Joseph, his adoptive father, proving that he was legal heir to the promises given Abraham and David. Luke 3 gives Mary's (Miryam's) genealogy, again showing Messiah's descent from David.

Furthermore, after Yeshua's death and ascension into heaven he took his seat "at the right hand of *HaG'dulah* [the majesty] in heaven" (Hebrews 8:1). Relevation 1:5 records John's declaration that Yeshua is "ruler of the kings of the earth."

Yeshua/Jesus was the son of David, the everlasting king.

The Miraculous Birth of the Messiah, Isaiah 7:14

Most Christians are familiar with the often-quoted Christmas prophecy:

> Behold, a virgin shall be with child, and shall bring forth a son, and they shall call his name Emmanuel, which being interpreted is, God with us. Matthew 1:23, KJV

Matthew, writing under the inspiration of the Holy Spirit, considers this prophecy, given to Isaiah, to have found its fulfillment in the miraculous birth of the Messiah. You need to be aware, however, that you may get some argument from your Jewish friend about the use of the word translated as "the virgin," *ha'alma*. Technically, *alma* means "young woman"; there is another Hebrew word, *betulah*, that specifically means "virgin."

Isaiah 7:14 is a valid and usable Messianic prophecy, but unless you engage in detailed study of the nature of this verse, it might be best to avoid it until you do. Scholars still disagree as to *how* Messiah's birth was a fulfillment of Isaiah's prophecy.

However, it might help your Jewish neighbor if you point out that God used miraculous births in the creation of the Jewish people. The "births" of Adam and Eve were miracles. The wives of Abraham, Isaac, and Jacob were all barren until God opened their wombs to bring forth the children of Israel.

It should come as no surprise that he used a miraculous birth to save his people, too. Bringing the Messiah through a virgin is perfectly consistent with the way the Almighty worked in times past. After all, as one eminent Jewish scholar said to me, "A virgin birth is a garden-variety miracle for God. After all, didn't he create the entire world?"

The Messiah's Incredible Name, Isaiah 9:6

The verse we just discussed, Isaiah 7:14, is found in a section that has been referred to as the "Book of Emmanuel." This rich portion of the book of Isaiah includes another great Messianic prophecy, Isaiah 9:6 (9:5 in Jewish bibles):

> For a child is born to us, a son is given to us; dominion will rest on his shoulders, and he will be given the name Pele-Yo'etz El Gibbor Avi-'Ad Sar-Shalom [Wonder of a Counselor, Mighty God, Father of Eternity, Prince of Peace].

This phenomenal prophecy describes the Messianic reign and attributes of the little baby who was later born in Bethlehem. No Jew in history could be described with these names, no Jew except Yeshua, the Messiah.

The Time of Messiah's Coming, Daniel 9:24–27

Soon after I was first confronted with the message of the Messiah, I struggled with a dilemma. I found myself beginning to believe the Gospel. This frightened me, because I knew if I professed belief in Jesus, it would change the course of the rest of my life.

I was still studying and practicing Transcendental Meditation, still expecting to become a teacher of this technique. Suddenly Yeshua entered the picture. If he was really the Messiah, I'd have to regroup, retrain, and redirect my life. It was a terrifying thought.

On top of this, I already suspected that although my parents and friends might not disown me, they certainly would disassociate from me. To some extent this happened. (This is not unusual for Jewish believers, but you should know that relationships with my family, after going through some upheaval, have become better than ever. I tell you this so you might help your Jewish neighbor deal with his or her possible fears.)

It was Thursday, the night of Dan Rigney's Bible study. Instead of continuing in Isaiah, we turned to Daniel. I felt a bit relieved, thinking that I was finally on familiar ground. Daniel, after all, was the one from the lion's den and the fiery furnace, the Daniel I had learned about when I was a child. I didn't know anything about Isaiah.

What I didn't know was that God had revealed to Daniel the precise timing of the coming of his Messiah. Wow! I thought as we entered into a study of Daniel 9. This will really clinch it for me. Verse 24 talked about a certain amount of time, after which the Messiah would come, transgression would be finished, iniquity would be atoned for, everlasting righteousness would be brought in, and an anointing (that's like saying a "Messiah-ing") of the most holy place would occur.

Verse 26 knocked me over. It said that in connection with this period the Messiah would be cut off—killed. Then, after the Messiah's death, the city (Jerusalem) and the sanctuary (the Temple) would be destroyed. Both Jerusalem and the Temple were destroyed in 70 C.E.! That meant the Messiah had to have died *before* 70 C.E.

Daniel 9 immediately brought me one step closer in making a decision to believe. But something else hit me at exactly the same time. If all this was as clear as it seemed to me, then why didn't the rabbis see it? I figured that I'd better get myself over to a rabbi before I fell for something that wasn't true. I realized that either my fellow Jews had, for the most part, missed the Messiah, or all my Christian friends were following a lie. I had to know.

Since I didn't really know any rabbis personally, I trekked over to my folks' house to find out if they did. My dad referred me to a rabbi in downtown Washington, D.C. I set up an appointment to talk with him. Bringing a Bible into his office I asked, "Rabbi, would you please explain to me the 'Jewish' interpretation of Daniel chapter 9?"

His response jolted me. "I advise you," he said, "not to study the Bible. When you do you get all confused."

"But Rabbi," I protested, "don't you believe in God?"

I will always remember his response. "God," he mused, "is a good hypothesis!"

I was shocked. When I left his office, I was so disoriented I couldn't find my car. I knew what I needed—a rabbi who truly believed in God and accepted the Bible as his Word. But I didn't know any Orthodox rabbis whom I could contact.

When I went to work the next day, a strange "coincidence" occurred. The front door opened and in walked a man I had never seen before. He had a long white beard and the dark clothing that identified him as an Orthodox rabbi. I just about jumped on him.

"Rabbi, I must study with you!" I cried out.

"Do you want to be a rabbi?" he asked.

I shook my head. "I don't know, I just want to know the truth."

The kind rabbi invited me to his home to study with him, and I did so for several months. When I asked him about Daniel 9 he simply said that he was not allowed to study that portion of Scripture, for it calculated the time of the coming of Messiah.

"So," I said, "why can't you study that?"

He looked solemn. "The *Talmud* forbids us to calculate the coming of the Messiah." This, he explained, was to prevent speculation and possible loss of faith should the Messiah not come at the calculated time.

Now I was convinced. If the old rabbi was right—that the verses in Daniel foretold the coming of the Messiah—and if the calculations I had already made were correct, Yeshua had to be the Messiah.

In sharing with your Jewish neighbor, it is not always necessary to go into great detail concerning these calculations. Often it is enough to show that there is a time period that concludes with the death of the Messiah (for the purpose of putting an end to iniquity) and that this time period is to be completed before the destruction of the Temple in 70 C.E.

Daniel 9, like Isaiah 53, is one of the most powerful of the Messianic prophecies.

The Messiah's Birthplace, Micah 5:2

Not only did God reveal why, how and when the Messiah would come, he also was specific about where he would be born. Micah 5:2 (5:1 in Jewish Bibles) reads:

> But you, Beit-Lechem near Efrat, so small among the clans of Y'hudah, out of you will come forth to me the future ruler of Isra'el, whose origins are far in the past, back in ancient times.

God chose a humble town for Messiah's birth—Bethlehem, the city of David.

Matthew refers to this verse in chapter 2 of his Gospel. When Herod gathered the chief priests and Scribes together and asked them where the Messiah was to be born, they quoted Micah 5:2. This prophecy was clearly considered Messianic in the days of Yeshua.

The Messiah's New Covenant, Jeremiah 31:31–33

Jewish people might challenge you about the New Testament: "Where were we told that we needed another Testament? Isn't one enough?" The answer to this question can be found in Jeremiah 31:31-33.

Through Jeremiah, God promised a new covenant to his people, different from the former covenant, the Mosaic covenant. Under the new covenant God promised to write his Law on the hearts of his people instead of just writing it on tablets of stone.

During his final Passover with his disciples, Messiah referred to the cup of wine he handed them to drink as the "new covenant" in his blood (Luke 22:20). When a person trusts the Messiah, the Law is written on his heart—a Law that also includes forgiveness for sin because of his perfect sacrifice.

This is not to imply that it's wrong to keep the commandments, even the very letter of the Law. The Law that God gave, extolled at great length in Psalm 119, is holy, just, and good, as Paul said (Romans 6:12). If, however, the Law is kept *only* externally, with a heart far from God, then observing the Law is less beneficial.

Having a trust relationship with God is the most important aspect of the spiritual life. Because of that relationship, a person will be committed to performing godly deeds. Following God's ways is a consequence of salvation, not a condition for salvation. I like to say that we strive to follow the law, not *for* salvation, but *from* salvation.

Jeremiah promised that a new covenant would someday shift the observance of God's Law from an external exercise to an internal instinct. And of course, this is a great blessing, for to follow the ways of God always meant receiving the blessings of God.

Presenting Messianic Prophecy

Now that you are armed with prophecies for presenting the Messiah to your Jewish neighbor, let me caution you. It's very important to be humble, yet firm, in your discussion of these prophetic passages. It's new and unfamiliar ground for most Jewish people. Further, there has been some valid criticism concerning the way these verses are sometimes used and interpreted.

Believers are accused of lifting verses of Scripture out of their historical context. To some extent that is true. It isn't that those portions are not Messianic prophecies. They are. But *how* they are Messianic is not so easily understood.

Nevertheless, do not hesitate to present Messianic prophecy in your effort to share the Gospel. Messianic prophecies are part of the Word of God and were given to help his people find the Messiah. Many testimonies of Jewish believers include reference to the passages we have examined here.These types of testimonies and more in-depth material on Messianic prophesies are available.

— 7 —

SEMANTICS & SENSITIVITIES

— or —

Building Bridges, Not Walls

I stood in front of a sea of blank faces. It was taking me a while to get the point across to my general semantics class at Howard University.

"The word is not the thing," I repeated once again. But somehow this basic principle of semantics was not hitting home. "For instance," I continued, "the word *dog* is not the dog itself. It is only a sound that stands for the animal—a 'symbol'; the dog itself is called the referent."

I then asked everyone in the class to draw a picture of a dog. Soon there were pictures of huge dogs and tiny dogs. Black dogs and white dogs. Mean-looking dogs and wimpy little dogs. Someone even drew a hot dog. The exercise finally got the point across. Words can sometimes be a poor form of communication, but they are the tools that we have to work with.

It's important to understand that, whereas a word may mean one thing to you, it will often convey a different meaning to someone else. In talking to your Jewish neighbor about Jesus, this principle is especially true. The issue is really a matter of "denotative" and "connotative" meanings.

The denotative meaning of a word is its original technical meaning. For example, the word *water*, denotatively, is "H_2O." Water is composed of two atoms of hydrogen and one atom of oxygen. That's its denotative meaning.

Connotatively, however, *water* means so much more. It might connote a summer's vacation at the beach. It might call forth the frustration of bailing out a flooded basement. It might evoke the pleasant memory of guzzling a big glass of it after mowing the lawn.

The word *water* carries both denotative and connotative meanings. The word *water* is not the thing itself.This is the nature of semantics. *The word is not the thing, it is a symbol that stands for the thing*.

Nowhere is this seen more clearly than in sharing the message of the Messiah with your Jewish neighbor.

The fellow in my Coast Guard Reserve unit witnessed to me using semantically sensitive language. His choice of words arrested my attention and got me to consider what he was saying.As I mentioned earlier, in answer to my question about that elusive peace he seemed to have captured, he smiled and said, "Your Messiah lives in my heart."

He used the term *Messiah*, derived from the Hebrew *Mashiach*, meaning "anointed one." In Greek, the word for *anointed* is *Christos*, commonly "Christ." Messiah and Christ mean exactly the same thing technically, or denotatively.They can both be defined by the single English word *anointed*. But, connotatively, they convey two entirely different meanings. Here is a classic case where the word is definitely not the thing.

To a Jewish person, Christ is the last name of the Gentile deity. I was surprised at how many non-Jewish Christians think that, too. To a Jewish person, Christ conducted the Crusades, invoked the Inquisition, and prompted the persecution of Jews over the last twenty centuries.To a Jewish person, Christ is the first part of the term used by those who accuse Jews of deicide: "Christ-killers!"

If that fellow in the Coast Guard had told me that "Christ lived in his heart," it would have meant something entirely different to me. I would have thought to myself, "Well, that's nice for you. You're supposed to believe that stuff. But it's got nothing to do with me. Maybe I should consider how to have more of Moses in my heart."

His whole point would have been lost because he did not use semantically sensitive language. Connotatively, in the mind of a Jewish person, *Christ* does not equal *Messiah*. Jewish people are more comfortable with the term Messiah, even though most Jews don't embrace a Messianic hope. (More on that in Section III.)

So, if you're talking about the anointed one, the Christ, why not say it the Jewish way—Messiah! It makes for more effective communication.

Christians use other semantically "loaded" terms in witnessing. Some terminology can be replaced with language that is less offensive, less ambiguous, and still makes the same point . . . only better.

The apostle Paul told the Corinthian believers, "Do not be an obstacle to anyone—not to the Jews, not to Gentiles, and not to God's Messianic Community [Church]" (I Corinthians 10:32) and ". . . what I did was put myself in the position of a Jew, in order to win Jews" (I Corinthians 9:20). Even though he was writing to a Gentile church, he was quick to advise them about effective communication.

All groups develop a jargon, a unique way of saying something. Those who conform to the ways the group uses the jargon are considered the "in group." Those who don't are considered "out." It is certainly not your goal to shut the door on your Jewish neighbor, making him or her feel excluded from the family of God. Instead, you want to use language to draw the person in, to truly communicate all that God has offered in Yeshua.

Words are the tools God has given us for communication. How much more effective we can be with skilled use of this precious tool!

I urge you to consider learning and using those words that are less offensive to Jews and that, at the same time, may more clearly communicate biblical truth. You will not just become a better communicator; you will also gain a new perspective on many of the doctrines of the faith.

The following list contains words that can be either confusing or objectionable to Jewish people. I have also attempted to explain the reason for suggesting the change.

Semantic Substitutes for a Sensitive Witness

1. Instead of using the description *Christian*, say *Messianic*, *biblical* or *scriptural*.

To a Jewish person, the adjective *Christian* does not describe a follower of the Messiah of Israel. It means someone who is a non-Jewish church-goer, Catholic, Episcopalian, Baptist, Presbyterian, etc.

It makes little difference if the person is "born again" or is even practicing the Christian faith. Being Jewish is a matter of birth, not choice. Therefore, being Christian is also seen as a matter of birth, not choice.

Messianic or *biblical* has the same meaning and communicates something Jewish.

EXAMPLE: "That was not a very biblical thing to do," instead of, "That was not a Christian thing to do." Or, "We follow the Messianic faith," rather than, "We are Christians."

2. Instead of calling someone a *Christian* try the term *believer*.

Christian means "one who follows Christ." To a Jew, *Christian* is equated with *Gentile* and has little to do with the Messiah or anything Jewish. That's why *believer* or *believer in Yeshua* is more communicative.

EXAMPLE: "I am a believer in the Messiah," instead of, "I am a Christian."

3. Instead of using the word *Christ*, use the term *Messiah*.

As explained already, *Christ* is not understood to mean "anointed one"; it is presumed, instead, to be the last name of the Gentile deity. *Messiah* is a more familiar word to represent the same person.

EXAMPLE: "I follow Yeshua, the Messiah." instead of "Jesus Christ is my Lord."

4. Instead of referring to your place of worship as a *church*, call it a *congregation*.

Although Church means "called-out body of believers"—Jews *and* Gentiles—to a Jew, a church is the place Gentiles gather to worship on Sunday. It is not something with which Jews are traditionally involved. A word that can be substituted is *congregation* since that is what most Jewish people call their place of worship.

EXAMPLE: "I just came back from services in my congregation," instead of, "I just came back from church."

5. Instead of using the Greek name *Jesus*, try calling the Messiah by the name he was called by his family and disciples: *Yeshua* (short for Yehoshua, or Joshua).

Many Jewish people have a hard time saying the name *Jesus*. Many were taught never to utter that name in their homes. Since his followers called him *Yeshua*, his Hebrew name, rather than *Jesus*, the Greek rendering of his name, it is acceptable to use his Hebrew name. Both names, one Greek, one Hebrew, denote the same thing—Savior. But connotatively, one is Jewish while the other is quite Gentile.

EXAMPLE: "Joseph and Miryam (you probably know her as Mary) had a son named Yeshua."

6. Instead of saying that Jesus *died for my sins*, try using the phrase *atoned for my sins*.

The word *atonement* is more familiar to Jewish people since the Day of Atonement is an annual observance. Yeshua's sacrifice was the fulfillment of this holy day. The message is clearer if you relate that fact in your witness.

EXAMPLE: "Messiah Yeshua atoned for my sins," instead of, "Christ died for my sins."

7. Instead of referring to the Comforter as the *Holy Spirit* or *Holy Ghost*, use the term *Spirit of God*.

Although the title *Holy Spirit* does appear in the Old Testament (*Holy Ghost* in the King James Version), to a Jewish ear it rings of Roman Catholicism. It also emphasizes the concept of the Trinity, a difficult idea even for Christians, but especially for Jews, to comprehend. *Spirit of God* is a term found in Genesis 1:2.

EXAMPLE: "He is filled with the Spirit of God," instead of, "He is filled with the Holy Ghost."

8. Instead of using the word *Trinity*, use the term *composite unity* or *tri-unity of God.*

The term *Trinity* is not found in Scripture. Coined at the Council of Nicea, it is a man-made attempt to describe the mysterious and unique nature of God; instead, the use of the term *Trinity* confuses the issue. (See Section IV.)

EXAMPLE: "We believe in the composite unity or tri-unity of God," instead of, "We believe in the Trinity."

9. Instead of calling the salvation message the *Gospel*, speak of it as the *Good News.*

To a Jew, the message of the *Gospel* has seemed like bad news, not good news. Those bearing the message have often persecuted Jews. It's good to define the word, since the term *Gospel* has only negative connotations.

EXAMPLE: "I am sharing the Good News that the Messiah came to atone for sin," instead of, "I am a minister of the Gospel of Jesus Christ."

10. Instead of celebrating *Easter*, emphasize the fact that it's *Resurrection Day.*

Easter connotes eggs, bonnets, parades, *and* anti-Semitism. As we have already mentioned, the name is derived from that of the pagan goddess Ishtar, and was picked up by the Church centuries ago. It has little to do with the concept of *resurrection*, which, as we will see in Section IV, *is* very Jewish.

EXAMPLE: "We are attending our Resurrection Day services," instead of, "We are going to Easter services."

11. Instead of using the word *Christmas*, why not call it *Messiah's birthday*?

Again, the word *Christmas* is associated with more than just the birth of the Messiah. It connotes tinsel, trees, Santa Claus. These are all pleasant traditions for Gentiles. They do not have much relevance for Jews. But the birth of Messiah is of critical importance to Jewish people.

EXAMPLE: "Happy Messiah's birthday," instead of "Merry Christmas."

12. Instead of *Pentecost*, refer to the holiday as *Shavu'ot.*

The holyday discussed in Acts 2 was known as *Shavu'ot* (pronounced Sha-voo-*ote*). *Pentecost* is the Greek way of saying it. To

Jewish people, when they hear about *Pentecost*, all they can think about is Pentecostalism and the extremes associated with that movement—snake handling and rolling in the aisles—something to which most Jews can't relate. But Pentecost was the Jewish holyday *Shavu'ot*.

EXAMPLE: "The believers were gathered for *Shavu'ot*," instead of, "The Christians were gathered for Pentecost."

13. Instead of looking forward to the *Second Coming of Christ*, how about anticipating the *return of the Messiah?*

Think how much more is communicated to Jewish people when you speak of the Messiah's return in a Jewish way. It puts his return to the Mount of Olives in its proper Jewish context.

EXAMPLE: "I look forward to the return of the Messiah," rather than, "I am awaiting the Second Coming of Christ."

14. Instead of calling the second portion of the Holy Scriptures the *New Testament*, another way to refer to it is the *New Covenant* or in Hebrew, *B'rit Chadashah*.

As you learned from the section on Messianic prophecy, God promised the Jewish people that he would make a "new covenant" with them. This term, in either English or Hebrew, will feel more relevant to your Jewish neighbor. The New Testament is seen as the Gentile portion of the Bible.

EXAMPLE: "This is found in the New Covenant," instead of "the New Testament."

15. Instead of calling the first part of the Bible the *Old Testament*, say *Tanakh* or *Hebrew Scripture*.

To a Jew, the portion of the Bible with which he is familiar is not old (as in decrepit). It is not much older than the Newer Testament. It can be condescending and offensive to call someone's holy book "old."

Tanakh includes *Torah* (the Five Books of Moses), *N'vi'im* (the prophets), and *K'tuvim* (the writings). This T-N-K acronym is how Jewish people refer to the "older" portion of the Bible. However, sometimes, it's called *Torah*, expanding the term beyond the five books of Moses.

EXAMPLE: "We are studying the *Tanakh*," rather than, "We are studying the Old Testament."

16. Instead of saying *baptism*, say *immersion* or *mikveh*—the ritual purification through bathing.

There are, of course, widely varying opinions among believers as to the prescribed mode of baptism. Nevertheless, for the sake of your Jewish friend or neighbor who cares little for the controversy but for whom the word *baptize* carries unpleasant connotations, why not substitute the word *immerse*? Regardless of your personal feelings about the preferred mode of baptism, it will represent a better point of identification with him.

If you will recall what I shared with you about the Jews during the Spanish Inquisition, you will understand why "baptism" is a sensitive word today. In Spain, Jews were forced to be baptized. It wasn't in response to true faith; it was the result of forced compliance.

The true origin of the act of baptizing goes back to the Jewish traditions associated with symbolic cleansing, today called *mikveh*. John the "Immerser" put his followers through this ceremony so they could symbolize their identification with his message and show their internal conviction to turn from sin. In like manner, being immersed in the name of Yeshua means identifying with his message.

EXAMPLE: Instead of saying, "I've just been baptized," say, "I've been immersed to show my identification with the Messiah."

17. Instead of saying *cross*, say *tree* or *altar* or even *execution stake*.

Although the cross represents the culmination of Yeshua's earthly ministry, people have ruined the real meaning of love that was demonstrated there. Instead of seeing the cross as the site of salvation, Jews now view it as a place of persecution. As we saw earlier, the cross is regarded with fear by Jewish people.

EXAMPLE: Instead of saying, "Jesus died on the cross for sin," say, "Yeshua atoned for sin on the execution stake."

18. Instead of saying *conversion*, say *completion* or *repentance.*

The Bible uses the term *conversion* to mean turning away from sin and toward God. But in our society, *conversion* has come to mean changing religions. When a Jew accepts Yeshua, he does not change religions, but he does turn from sin and toward God.

EXAMPLE: Instead of saying "converted Jew," say "completed Jew," "repentant Jew" or even "Messianic Jew"—a term used by Jewish believers.

This list is by no means exhaustive. But it offers you the prime examples of words and phrases that can be modified to bring the Good News of Salvation closer to the heart of your Jewish neighbor. By making these small adjustments in speech, you will not only be taking into account the connotative meanings of these emotionally charged words, but you will also gain further insight into the Jewish roots of your own faith.

Now that you're familiar with Messianic terminology, why don't we put into practice what you've just learned? We will use Messianic terminology exclusively throughout the rest of the book. It will give you an opportunity to feel more comfortable using this sensitized language.

SECTION III

The Audience: Your Jewish Neighbor

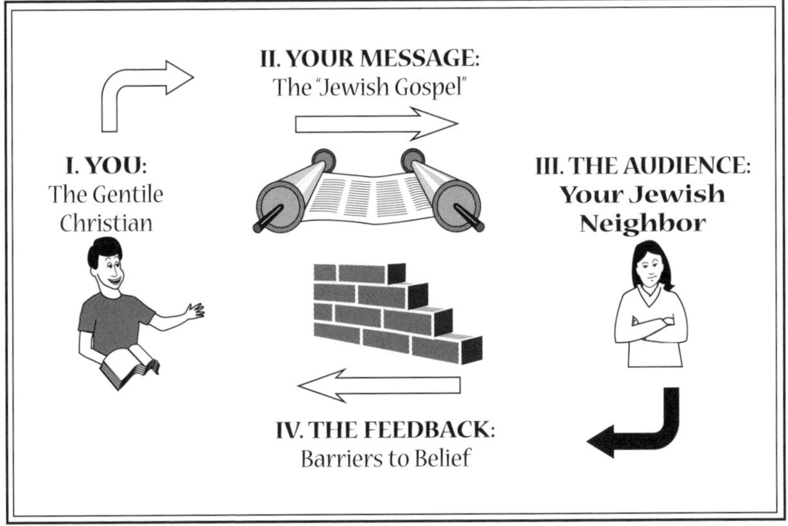

A friend of mine used to sell jewelry. Once, when we were discussing ways to communicate the message of the Messiah more effectively, she said that in sales the words she lived by were "Know your customer!" I can affirm that this is true because of a transaction I had with a car salesman.

It was time for us to buy a new car. Steffi was still driving the Volvo we had purchased right after getting married in 1975. Although we finally contributed the car to an organization that repaired older vehicles and gave them to Russian Jewish immigrants, she needed something more suited to her life as a suburbanite with two children who have lots of friends and places to go.

We decided to check out the new mini-vans and headed for our nearest dealer. Four years earlier, I had purchased a car at that very place; it was the car we were now trading in on the van. I still remembered the salesman who had persuaded me to spend thousands of dollars on that little car. He was an *m.o.t.*, a member of the tribe. In other words, he was Jewish.

An unusual thing about this particular dealership is that it is owned and run predominantly by Arabs. But they have a few Jewish salesmen and it was one of these who had helped me purchase the car. This same salesman approached us now as we returned to buy the van.

I was impressed that he remembered my name. "Mr. and Mrs. Rubin, how nice to see you again! How are your two lovely daughters?"

I liked him! Right away, I was ready to buy! I still can't figure out how he remembered our names. Do they keep photos of customers and spend each morning memorizing faces? How *do* they *do* it?

Anyway, the man had taken pains to "know his customer."

This is a basic principle of all good communication. In classes on public speaking and persuasion, the importance of "audience analysis" is always stressed.

Few examples of this stand out more than John F. Kennedy's *Ich bin ein Berliner* speech. Sensing the need to identify with his German audience, Kennedy spoke in German, referring to himself as their fellow countryman. As a result, he brought the house down. He knew his audience and identified with them. They loved him.

This section will introduce you to your Jewish neighbors. You may know their names. You may know the names of their children. You may even have established a comfortable relationship, sharing some of the intimate details of your lives. But there's always room to learn more, right?

I hope these chapters will dispel some common misconceptions you might have about Jewish people and help you better understand Jewish history, religion, culture, and values.

So here goes. Let me introduce you to your Jewish neighbor!

— 8 —

MISCONCEPTIONS ABOUT JEWISH PEOPLE

— or —

All Jews Aren't Created Equal

Stereotypes can be easily etched in one's mind and can be quite damaging. Stereotypes about blacks, about women, about the elderly, and even about children have caused serious problems in our society.

Stereotypes about Jews present another unique problem. They have precipitated a situation that has seriously hampered the spread of the Good News among God's chosen people.

In this chapter I hope to dispel some of these stereotypes, these misconceptions, in an attempt to enhance your understanding of your Jewish neighbor. To make it easier, these misconceptions will be divided into two sections—personal and spiritual.

Personal Misconceptions

If someone were asked to describe the physical characteristics of a Jew, it would not be surprising to hear references to a large nose, short stature, and curly black hair. Where these stereotypes originated, I do not know. The truth is that not all Jews have big noses. Not all Jews are short. Not all Jews have curly black hair. Stereotypes are just not always true.

If someone were asked to describe the behavioral characteristics of the Jewish people, the words *stingy* and *bookish* might come to mind. Perhaps it was Shakespeare's Shylock or Dickens' Fagin that gave rise to the "stingy" myth. It is true that one Jew, Jack Benny, deliberately exaggerated this stereotype. (Jack Benny was really not a tightwad; he was one of the most generous men in Hollywood.)

Jews are not stingier than other people. In fact, Jewish people are downright philanthropic, giving more to charities, per capita, than most other people.

The stereotype of the Jewish intellectual may stem from the many Jews who have made contributions to the academic fields. As a general rule, education *is* emphasized in the homes of Jewish families, but the same can be said of other groups. In addition, of course, not all Jews are highly educated.

The source of these stereotypes is not really important for our purposes. What remains for us is to understand that stereotypes and misconceptions will not help you know your Jewish neighbor, and may actually hinder your ability to communicate the Good News to him or her.

This is probably not a revelation to you. Anyone interested enough in Jewish people to get this book would likely add a resounding "amen" to these thoughts. And though you may not indulge in "Jewish" jokes or revert to habits of personal stereotyping, there often remain, even among believers, certain misconceptions about the Jewish people. These usually surface when it comes to the discussion of spiritual issues.

Spiritual Stereotypes

Not long ago, while I was conducting a seminar on sharing the Messiah with Jewish people, I was asked a question by one of the church members: "What do Jews think the Messiah will be like?" It seemed a logical question raised by a believer who wanted to better understand his Jewish neighbor. My answer shocked the audience.

I explained that most Jews don't believe in the coming of a personal Messiah. The participants could hardly believe their ears. Certainly, they supposed, the people to whom the Messiah was promised would be awaiting his appearance.

Sadly, today's Jews have little or no concern for the coming of a personal Messiah. After the Holocaust, many Jews lost hope. Certainly there are some who still do believe, but for those Jews who deny a personal Messiah, but still want to hold some hope, a "Messianic age" concept has developed. This is the belief that humankind will "evolve" into a higher state of consciousness. That was the view I held when I jumped into Transcendental Meditation.

The misconception that Jews believe in the coming Messiah has led to some real problems in the witness of many believers. Believing that all one has to do is share a few rightly applied Messianic prophecies, a believer may find himself up against an unexpected shrug of apathy. The fact is, your Jewish neighbor is not sitting around waiting for the Messiah—wondering where he will be born, who his ancestors will be, or what his ministry will accomplish.

Many believers, therefore, find themselves answering questions their Jewish neighbors have never even thought of, much less asked. It takes a while to earn enough trust to talk about personal things like a relationship with God. You can't just jump into Messianic prophecy. The conclusion of this book—"Putting It All Together"—will talk about this in greater detail. For now, though, you need to understand that although you may be absolutely clear on how to present Messiah in the *Tanakh*, your Jewish friend might simply say, "Well, I don't believe in the Messiah, anyway." In fact, you might hear something like this: "And I don't believe the Bible is God's Word, either."

Perhaps you've always assumed that all Jewish people share the same theology. Nothing could be further from the truth. Along with varying degrees of Bible knowledge and differing Messianic expectations, you will find that Jewish people hold extremely diverse opinions about God, the afterlife, Israel, and most other subjects.

These next chapters should help you get to know your Jewish neighbor in the areas of history, religion, and culture. They are designed to provide you with an overview and will, therefore, be general. Certainly not all of the information will apply to *your* Jewish neighbor. Remember all we said about stereotyping and misconceptions. So, forewarned and forearmed, let's take a look at the history of the Jewish people.

— 9 —

A BRIEF HISTORY OF THE JEWISH PEOPLE

— or —

The Wanderings of the Wandering Jews

To condense 4,000 years of history into a few pages is an impossible task. This would be true even if the people under consideration led routine lives. But Jews! A community that has heard the voice of God, a nation that has been in nearly every country, a people from whom the Messiah came—no, condensing the history of the Jews is not easy. But some history is necessary to help you in your witness.

We'll begin with the assumption that you are somewhat familiar with biblical Jewish history from years of sermons and Sunday school lessons. So we will focus primarily on post-biblical times. A few key biblical events, however, should be laid out as a foundation for the rest.

From Abraham to the Babylonian Captivity: The Beginnings of the Jewish Nation and the First Commonwealth

The Jewish people began when God called Abram out of Ur of the Chaldees. His willingness to respond to God's call was indicative of his great faith. God chose to bless Abram, changing his name to Abraham, "The father of a multitude," promising that his descendants would be as numerous as the stars in the heaven and the dust of the earth.

This people continued through Abraham's son Isaac, and Isaac's son Jacob. The nation grew in number when the Jews lived in Egypt, where they became slaves. God, however, remembering his covenant, planned to bring them to the land he had promised to the patriarchs. With Moses as deliverer, the people were led out of bondage and into freedom.

Moses is affectionately called *Moshe Rabbeynu*, "Moses our teacher." He is held in the highest esteem, not only as a great teacher of truth, as evidenced in the *Torah*, but as the one who led the Jewish people out of bondage. On Passover, an annual celebration that even the most secular Jews generally observe, Moses is mentioned many times. Referring to the patriarchs or Moses will place your Jewish neighbor on familiar territory, and the two of you on common ground.

After Moses died, Joshua led the people into the Promised Land. They entered with the *Torah*—the Law, the set of rules and regulations for life in the land God had given them. The people, having heard all that God required, had ratified the covenant, promising to do what the Lord had demanded.

Upon entering the Promised Land, Israel had to conquer the many nations living there. Joshua led the conquest and, following his death, Israel was ruled by the Judges. All the while, the Jewish people encountered tremendous opposition to their right to live in the Promised Land.

Soon, the temptation to mix with the surrounding nations and to adopt some of their practices caused the Jews further problems. An example of this is the way in which Israel was to be governed. Although it was clear that God wanted to remain the unique king of Israel, the Jewish people, surrounded by earthly monarchies, demanded that God provide for them a human king.

The first king, Saul, turned out to be a disaster for the Jewish people. God had warned them this would happen. In his grace, as a replacement for Saul, he provided a decent—although not perfect—king for his people. That king was David.

Through David, God revealed many truths to his people, some concerning David's future descendant, Yeshua. It was David whom the Lord used to bring forth many psalms that point to the Messiah—among them Psalm 2, Psalm 22, and Psalm 110. These can be used as Messianic prophecies, but because David is known as a poet, not a prophet, they might be subject to question.

After the reign of David and his son Solomon came the period of the Kings. The Jewish nation had become divided into the northern kingdom, known as Israel, and the southern kingdom, called Judah. Both kingdoms wandered into pagan ways, in spite of the prophetic messages God sent them. Although the primary purpose of the prophets was to realign the people of Israel with God's original plan and purpose, the prophets also shared predictions from God, prophetic messages concerning the coming Messiah.

In 721 B.C.E., the northern kingdom was taken into captivity by Assyria as a punishment for walking in ways of ungodliness. In 586 B.C.E. the southern kingdom, too, was taken captive by the Babylonians. The Jews were no longer in the Promised Land. It was during this period of captivity that God raised up prophets to give the people hope and guidance. Daniel, the one through whom God revealed the time of Messiah's coming, prophesied during this period.

From the Babylonian Captivity to the Great Dispersion: The Second Commonwealth

The *soferim,* the scribes, occupied high governmental positions during the monarchical period. Later, without kings to assist, they were free to delve more deeply into the study of the Law of Moses and the writings of the Jewish people. Ezra was described as "scribe of the Law of the God of heaven," equivalent to our Secretary of Education. The office of scribe replaced the office of prophet in religion. The influence of the scribes grew during the post-exilic period and through the first century of the Common Era.

The authority of the *rabbi* also began to develop following the Babylonian exile. Even after Ezra led in the construction of the second Temple in 517–516 B.C.E. (Solomon's Temple had been destroyed 70 years earlier), when the Jews were allowed to return to Israel and resume Temple worship, many chose to remain in exile, in the *galut*. Some Jewish men devoted themselves to the study of the *Torah*, and by the first century B.C.E., the rabbinic office had become well-established. The rabbis were not merely teachers, but spiritual authorities for their own disciples.

During these exilic and post-exilic periods, the oral traditions of the rabbis began to gain influence over the life of the ordinary Jew. Although these traditions were not officially compiled until several hundred years later (in a codification called the *Talmud*, or "oral law") they were recognized as authoritative for guiding the behavior of Jews well before the days of Yeshua.

Remembering that the oral law had been around for a while is essential to understanding the *B'rit Chadashah*, as well as sharing Yeshua with your Jewish neighbor. Many of the questions asked of Yeshua had to do with this oral tradition.

With the rise to power of the Greeks, under Alexander the Great, and later the Syrians, the Jews became dominated by other Gentile rulers. In 171 B.C.E., Antiochus IV, the leader of the Syrian-Greeks, began a direct assault on the Jewish way of life. He forbade circumcision and *Torah* study, and required obeisance to himself by giving himself the title *Epiphanes*, meaning "God-manifest." Many Jews refused to bow down to him. When he sacrificed a pig on the altar in the second Temple and dedicated the altar to the god Jupiter, a group of Jewish people became completely enraged.

A Jewish revolt began in Israel when Mattathias, a righteous priest, slew a fellow Jew for submitting to the ungodly commands of Antiochus. After three years of fighting led by Mattathias' son, Judah, the small band of Maccabees ("hammers") led the Jewish people to victory. They purged and rededicated the sacred Temple, which Antiochus had desecrated.

This is the story celebrated today as *Hanukkah*, Hebrew for "dedication." Not only is this battle recorded in the *Apocrypha*, the non-canonical writings of the Jews of the second Temple period, but the eighth chapter of the prophet Daniel paints a vivid picture of the events leading up to the Maccabean revolt. We know that Yeshua observed the anniversary of this military victory, for John 10:22 records his walking in the Temple at "the Feast of Dedication."

After the cleansing and rededication of the second Temple, two major political/religious parties developed in Israel, One, the party of the Scribes, known as Pharisees, were pietistic and separatistic. They began to lose control over the people, while their opponents, the Sadducees, who were more Hellenistic (influenced by Greek thinking), became more powerful. Life in Israel became a real mix of ideas, politics, the supernatural and the study of the *Torah* and prophets, combined with the traditions of the rabbis. And on top of this confusion was the increasing control of Rome.

During the first century of the Common Era, Roman rule dominated Jewish history. At the time of Yeshua, the Jews longed for a military Messiah, a hero like Judah Maccabee. It was this desire that caused so many to miss the truth that Yeshua was the Messiah; he just did not fulfill the people's expectation of a military leader. In fact, nothing in Jewish tradition taught that Messiah was to die and be resurrected. That is why he had to teach this to his disciples.

The number of synagogues in Israel had greatly increased by the first century. They were more a place for social gathering and study than for worship and ceremony. The Temple was still the focal point for Jewish worship. But with the complete destruction of the Temple in 70 C.E., some major changes took place.

The synagogue became the place of worship. Those Jews who had chosen to follow Yeshua, having understood him to be the fulfillment of the ancient sacrificial system of Israel, could not fit into the new rabbinic religion of Israel. The rabbis attempted to teach alternative means for atonement and to find explanations for the missing Temple. The Jewish believers could not submit to their teaching.

Furthermore, as we have said, Yeshua had warned his disciples to flee from the coming destruction of the Temple and Jerusalem (Matthew 24). Because of his teaching, the believers had removed themselves from a key event in Jewish history. The separation between the Jewish believers in Yeshua and the larger Jewish community was widening.

In 132 C.E., the gap grew greater still when the leading rabbi, Rabbi Akiva, proclaimed Bar Kokhba, a military leader, to be the Messiah. Believing him to be the military hero they sought, the Jewish authorities expected Bar Kokhba to lead the Jews in their revolt against Roman rule. After three years of struggle, this false Messiah led 580,000 Jews, including himself and Rabbi Akiva, to their deaths.

In 135 C.E., the Romans threw the Jews out of their land, dispersing them throughout the Roman Empire into Spain, Africa, Asia Minor, Europe, and elsewhere. This Diaspora has only really ended in the twentieth century. Keep in mind that some Jews did remain in the land of Israel, mostly in Galilee, but those who remained were very much in the minority from that time forth. Also, there were still Jews living in Babylon (today, Iraq) from the time of captivity.

Solomon Grayzel in *A History of the Jews* gives us information about Jewish population at that time.

> A reasonable guess estimates that there were about eight million Jews in the world just before the conflict with Rome. Probably about one million lived in Babylonia, outside the Roman empire.... Thus it has been calculated that in the first century C.E. the Jews were ten percent of the total population of the Roman empire.

The flight of the Jewish believers at the time of the destruction of the Temple, combined with their unwillingness to submit to rabbinic authority (particularly in the abandoning of the regular Jewish army under the command of Bar Kokhba), caused a permanent and total separation between them and the rest of the Jewish community.

We have record of Jewish believers leading congregations until the Council of Nicea in 325 C.E. After that time and the promulgation of the laws of the Theodosian Code, we see a disappearance of Jewish believers. Since that time, believers in Yeshua have often assimilated into predominately Gentile congregations.

This information can help you understand why it seems most Jews haven't believed in Yeshua through the ages. The fact is, many have, but because those Jewish believers did not remain part of the Jewish community, no one knew about them. Not until the recent revival among Jewish people and, with it, the rise of the Messianic congregational movement, has the Jewish community become aware that many Jews do believe in Yeshua.

From the Great Dispersion to Today

Because this is a book about sharing the Messiah with Jewish people, and not a modern history of the Jews, I've taken pains to choose those events that will most directly affect your witness. These five major events are:

1. The development of the *Talmud* and the Jewish religion
2. The anti-Semitism of the Roman Catholic Church
3. The immigration of Jews to the United States
4. The persecution by Nazi Germany
5. The rebirth of the nation of Israel

Our next chapter will discuss the *Talmud* in light of its impact upon Jewish religion. An earlier chapter spoke about the anti-Semitism of some of the Church fathers and of the Roman Catholic Church. What remains for us here is to consider the immigration of Jews to America, the Holocaust initiated by Nazi Germany, and the rebirth of Israel.

Jewish life in Europe in the second millennium was most unpleasant. Jews, as I said, were accused of causing the Black Death. They were blamed for many social, financial, and political problems. They began to be "ghetto-ized"— forced to live only among themselves.

Religious persecution persisted, and when there was an opportunity to move to America, where freedom seemed possible, many Jews packed up all they had, boarded boats, and sailed to the New World.

Although there have been Jews in this country since 1621, the first Jewish settlement wasn't officially established until 1654. As you might guess, it was in New Amsterdam, later known as New York.

Soon after, Jews came from many European countries, including Holland, England, Germany, and Spain. They had to struggle for their rights in this new land, but struggle they did. They fought in the American Revolution, won the right to own property, and were granted full U.S. citizenship equal to their Gentile counterparts.

By 1825, the United States had become home for 6,000 Jews. By the Civil War, mostly as a result of immigration, 150,000 Jews lived in the U.S. Like other Americans, some fought for the North, some for the South. By 1871, 250,000 Jews, mostly of German background, lived in this country.

During the period from 1881 to 1914, a second major wave of Jewish immigration washed across the American shore. These 2,000,000 Jews from Eastern and Central Europe were driven from their homeland by prejudice and pogroms. Most were Yiddish-speaking Orthodox Jews. During World War I, more than 250,000 Jews fought in the armed forces of the United States.

With the Jewish population growing, groups such as the Zionist Organization of America, the American Jewish Committee, the American Jewish Congress, and the Anti-Defamation League of B'nai B'rith were organized to tend to the needs of these new American citizens. The Great Depression brought extra pressure on this poor immigrant people.

Perhaps the single most important factor prompting Jews to escape to America was the rise of Hitler's virulent brand of anti-Semitism in Europe. Seeking safety, thousands of Jews emigrated before the dark days of destruction that began in 1933 when Hitler became dictator of Germany.

Hitler initiated a boycott of Jewish-owned businesses, confiscated the possessions of many Jews, and espoused a racial superiority doctrine. His policies were permitted under the Nuremberg Laws and promulgated by a powerful propaganda machine, particularly through widespread distribution of the newspaper *Der Sturmer*.

Hitler reasoned rightly that centuries of anti-Semitic propaganda would sufficiently affect and infect Western minds so that not many who heard of the horror would defend the Jews, no matter what the Nazis did. The *Protocols of the Elders of Zion*, a little booklet first printed in Czarist Russia, which Hitler had translated into German, detailed a Jewish plot to take over the world. It was later proven to be a fabricated document, but by then was already widely circulated, helping Hitler's cause. Henry Ford was one very influential

American who supported this poisonous propaganda until he admitted he had been misled. This book is reappearing in Moslem countries today.

The night of November 9–10, 1938, brought with it the horror of *Kristallnacht*, "the night of the broken glass." Hitler's hordes were unleashed; they destroyed synagogues, devastated Jewish shops and homes, and arrested thousands. The world remained silent.

From 1939 until the end of Hitler's horrors, 6,000,000 Jews and an equal number of non-Jews lost their lives under Nazi domination. During the time from 1933 to 1942, 175,000 Jews from Germany, Austria, and other Nazi-dominated lands escaped to enter the United States. Many more Jews arrived after World War II.

By 1957, the U.S. Jewish population had reached 5,200,000. Today that number is close to 6,000,000, with half living in the Greater New York City area. A half-million Jewish people reside in Los Angeles, a third of a million in Philadelphia, and several hundred thousand each in Boston, Chicago, and the Baltimore-Washington area.

About 4,000,000 Jews currently reside in Israel, hundreds of thousands from the former Soviet Union. The other four million Jews are scattered over all parts of the earth. This dispersion can be seen as the fulfillment of the word spoken by Moses: "*Adonai* will scatter you among all peoples from one end of the earth to the other" (Deuteronomy 28:64).

Without question, the single most important event in post-biblical Jewish history has been the rebirth of the state of Israel. Each year for nearly 2,000 years, Jewish people have concluded the Passover meal, by saying, "Next year in Jerusalem." This prayer, begun in 135 C.E., has been a plea to God to allow us to celebrate the Passover in Israel. In 1948, this longing became a reality.

Although Jews have inhabited Israel off and on since the Dispersion, it wasn't until the late 1800s that the notion of a renewed Jewish state began to receive support. Backed by funds supplied by Baron Edmond de Rothschild, Jews began to establish agricultural communities in Israel. In 1897, at the First Zionist Congress, convened by Theodor Herzl, the World Zionist Organization was founded to establish a homeland for the Jewish people in the land known today as Israel. Herzl was its first president.

Controversy raged within and without the worldwide Jewish community; still Herzl maintained his vision and obtained support for his cause from other leaders. Chaim Weizmann, the fourth president of the World Zionist Organization, was able to persuade England to issue the Balfour Declaration in 1917, approving the idea of a Jewish homeland in "Palestine."

It was not until 1948 that Israel was finally granted full statehood. Great Britain, receiving enormous pressure following World War II, opted to turn over the question of a Jewish state to the United Nations. The U.N. recommended dividing the territory into Israeli and Arab states. On May 14, 1948, Israel became a nation for the first time in modern history.

Although Israel has had to defend herself in numerous wars since 1948, it appears that in God's timing, the day for Israel to exist as a nation had come. It is a modern miracle that such a small country, vastly outnumbered by surrounding enemies, survives. We see this as God's hand protecting his people.

This skeletal report on 4,000 years of Jewish history has been designed to provide you with information to enhance your understanding of your Jewish neighbor. The next chapters will flesh out our skeleton by offering insight into the religion and culture of the Jewish people. They are tied very closely to the history that has been outlined thus far, and you will see the details of the completed picture come to life as we proceed.

— 10 —

THE RELIGION OF THE JEWISH PEOPLE

— or —

The Three T's: Torah, Temple & Talmud

In the study of civilizations it is usually quite difficult to separate history from religion. For the Jewish people it is impossible.

Why? Because the Jews were created with religion in mind. When God formed this people, his intention was that they would teach the world about him. From the beginning, the history and religion of the Jewish people were intertwined the way ivy crawls up amidst the branches of a tree.

The last chapter briefly surveyed the history of the Jewish people, from God's ancient covenant with Abraham to the establishment of the modern State of Israel. Throughout, there were references to religion. This chapter will highlight the religion of the Jewish people from Bible times, through its development over the last two millennia, and as it is practiced today.

From Abraham to the Great Dispersion

From the time of Abraham until the giving of God's Law through Moses, the religion of Israel was rather primitive. Altars of stone were erected to commemorate certain divine interventions by the Lord. Abram built an altar to the Lord upon receiving the promise of a land to be given to his descendants (Genesis 12:7). This practice seems rudimentary, but it was a great step up from the polytheism that marked the times.

With the revelation of the *Torah* on Mount Sinai, Israel's religion became oriented toward social relationships and the worship of God. The system of sacrifice became more developed. Through the Tabernacle and its later replacement, the Temple,

God revealed to his people an earthly picture of the heavenly courts (Hebrews 9:23).

Then, when Solomon's Temple was destroyed and the Jews were taken into captivity (586 B.C.E.), their religion changed dramatically. As the review of history indicated, the center of religious life now shifted. The scribes and their teachings dominated for nearly a century until the building of the second Temple, when emphasis returned to the ancient system of sacrifice prescribed by God, through Moses. But by the time the new Temple had been completed, the priesthood had taken on the nuances of a political rather than a religious office.

Amidst these changes, the rabbis gained greater authority. Various schools of religious philosophy developed and the Jewish people found themselves divided, as individuals allied themselves with one school or the other. By Yeshua's day there were the religious sects—Pharisees, Sadducees, and Essenes—and political sects like the Zealots. These are just a few of the many sects which divided the Jewish people.

The New Covenant talks much about the Pharisees and the Sadducees, both continually struggling for influence. The Pharisees were more flexible with regard to interpreting the Word of God, whereas the Sadducees were more literal in their interpretations, more rigid in their rules. The Pharisees believed in the reality of the supernatural, while the Sadducees denied it. An example of their divergent views is recorded in Matthew 22:23–33, in regard the question of the Resurrection. The Pharisees believed in resurrection; the Sadducees did not.

Another religious sect, the Essenes, had much in common with the early believers in the Messiah, particularly in that they shared all their earthly possessions. This separatist group was "heavenly" minded, hoping for a deliverer, but most likely did not follow Yeshua. Many scholars believe that the Essenes were the people responsible for preserving what are now called the Dead Sea Scrolls. Some have suggested that John (*Yochanan*, in Hebrew) the Immerser was a member of the Essenes.

In addition to these religious sects, there was also a party known as the Zealots. They were not truly religious, except in their dedication to overthrowing the Roman rule over Israel.

Judaism in the first century, and even somewhat earlier, had no clear-cut theology. Although many beliefs were held in common, there were also many variant viewpoints.

One conviction that many held in common, however, was that Yeshua was not the Messiah. Those who believed in him were considered a separate sect and were sometimes called "Nazarenes," sometimes "the Way," and sometimes "Christians" (although the "Greek-ness" of the term, in that the word "Christ" is present, instead of Messiah, seems to indicate that it was reserved mostly for Gentile followers of Yeshua).

From the Great Dispersion to Modern Times

In the last chapter, I mentioned the *Talmud*. More than anything else, this collection of writings influenced the religion of the Jewish people. In many ways, it *was* the religion of the Jewish people.

Referred to as the Oral Law, or the Tradition of the Elders, the *Talmud* is believed by many Jews to have been handed down on Mt. Sinai along with the written Law, the *Torah*. As a result, it has exerted tremendous influence in matters of religion.

The traditions and commentaries that later formed the *Talmud* trace their roots back into early Jewish history. Tradition teaches that Moses himself first received these oral laws, then passed them on to Joshua, who, in turn, handed them down to the elders (the judges). Then the laws were delivered to the prophets, who handed them over to the care of the Great Assembly, 120 leaders who returned from exile under the leadership of Ezra. This is according to *Avot*—a tractate of the *Talmud*—chapter 1. Finally the laws arrived in the hands of the rabbis.

Rabbi Akiva was responsible for organizing much of this oral material shortly after the time of the New Covenant. The writing, however, is credited to another, Rabbi Judah HaNasi. His work, known as the *Mishnah*, formed the foundation of what later became known as the *Talmud*. The Mishnah is not a commentary on the Bible, but rather is material organized in six sections, called Orders, which discuss various issues in the Bible and Jewish life. The teachers of Mishnah, called *Tanna'im*, completed their work around the end of the second century.

The rest of the *Talmud*, known as *Gemara*, was not completed until the end of the fifth century of the Common Era. The Gemara contains discussions concerning the Mishnah, conducted by the *Amora'im*, other Jewish scholars.

This entire system is predicated on the premise that God revealed the oral law to Moses, as well as the written law. Although it is rare to meet someone today who holds this elevated view of the *Talmud*, the impact of the traditions and teachings of the *Tanna'im* and the *Amora'im* must not be underestimated.

These teachers endeavored to construct a fence around the *Torah* to keep their people from violating the laws of Moses. By doing so, they hoped their people would not even get close enough to the laws to break them. The legal system became so cumbersome that rabbis were continually called upon to decide legal issues. That is why rabbis are sometimes called "lawyers" in the New Covenant.

In theory, the rabbis had a good idea. Sadly, though, people became so entangled in the multitude of rules and religious regulations that some of the essential meanings in the *Torah* became lost. Tradition overshadowed truth.

Yeshua spoke of this problem. In the Sermon on the Mount, he prefaced his "You have heard it said" remarks by instructing his disciples to exceed the righteousness of the scribes and the Pharisees. Stating specifically that he had come not to abolish the Law and the prophets, but rather to fulfill them, Yeshua then launched into a sermon on the essence of the Law. One can't help thinking that Yeshua's concern was to confront the authority of the oral tradition and to return his disciples to the deeper meaning of the *Torah*.

But the influence of the *Talmud* grew still greater. Different *Talmuds* developed in both Jerusalem and Babylon. Through the last 2,000 years, study of *Talmud* has been considered one of the noblest and highest practices to which a Jewish boy could commit himself. Its study has occupied the greatest minds of the Jewish people.

Much can be learned about the Bible from studying the writings in the *Talmud*. Much can be learned about Jewish history by reading the many debates and discussions recorded there. Unfortunately, even though some of the material found in the *Talmud* points to the Messiah, to a great extent its writings have obscured the Messiah from many Jewish eyes. Yeshua's view of the authority of the oral law, which is that it is not inspired as is the written law, coupled with his decision to delegate spiritual authority to his apostles, rather than the traditional rabbis, created a conflict that exists to this day.

Modern Times

Early Jewish settlers in the United States formed synagogues in which to worship. The first was founded in Newport, Rhode Island, in 1658. Later, synagogues were established in Savannah, Philadelphia, Charleston, and throughout the thirteen colonies. These were Orthodox synagogues. At that time no other branch of Judaism existed.

As the German Jews arrived in America in the mid-1800s, they brought with them the influence that led to Reform Judaism. Reform Judaism gleaned some of its ideology from the higher criticism of the German intellectual community, the same higher criticism that gave birth to the theological liberal movement within Christianity. In 1875 the Reform movement established the first U.S. rabbinical seminary, Hebrew Union College, in Cincinnati, Ohio, to develop and promote liberal Judaism.

In 1886 the Jewish Theological Seminary of America was formed in Philadelphia. From its teachings sprung another movement known as Conservative Judaism. Conservative Judaism rose up to moderate the Reform movement. It is theologically more conservative, more middle-of-the road, a compromise between Orthodox and Reform Judaism.

The fourth branch of Judaism is known as Reconstructionist Judaism. Originated by Mordecai Kaplan in 1934, it teaches that Judaism is more than a religion; it is a religious civilization. Although fewer in number than the other branches, Reconstructionism has some strong support within the intellectual circles of the Jewish people and is a growing movement.

Orthodox Jews strive to keep the laws and traditions of Judaism with great zeal. They express an expectancy for the coming Messiah. They believe in an afterlife and consider the *Torah* and *Talmud* to be the Word of God.

Reform Jews tend to liberalize laws and traditions, picking and choosing what they wish to believe and observe in today's world. They do not teach about the coming Messiah, but have opted for the concept of the Messianic age, a higher plane and a period of peace, into which they believe we are all moving.

Conservative Jews follow the teachings of the rabbis but allow for certain modifications to make tradition fit into the society in which it is practiced. For example, whereas Orthodox Jews do not allow men and women to sit together in the synagogue, Conservative Jews do. This middle-of-the-road position also guides their views pertaining to the Messiah and the afterlife.

Reconstructionist Jews, like Conservative Jews, seek to adapt Judaism to the world in which it must function. However, to this end Reconstructionist Jews, unlike Conservative Jews, incorporate modern secular thought in the services of their synagogues. They are drawn to concepts such as ethical culture, ritual enrichment, and artistic creativity.

It will help you in your witness to know a little about the various branches of Judaism, though you should not necessarily conclude that your neighbor is committed to all the doctrines espoused by the synagogue to which he belongs. As is the case with many Christians in churches, Jewish people often join synagogues, not so much because of theology, but because of proximity to their home and the personality of the rabbi. When you're getting to know your Jewish neighbor, at some point you'll want to ask what exactly he or she believes *personally*.

The glossary at the end of this book lists terms that pertain to the religious observances of the Jewish people. You will find that no matter which branch of Judaism your Jewish neighbor belongs to, most of the terms listed are relevant to one degree or another.

Take, for example, the term *kosher*, which means "acceptable" (to God). Most obvious, pork and shellfish are non-*kosher*, or *treyfe*. Generally, only the Orthodox and some Conservative Jews "keep *kosher*." But they may have their own individual interpretations.

An Orthodox Jew would not even go to a restaurant that served *treyfe*. However, a conservative Jew might not eat sweet-and-sour shrimp at home, but might in a Chinese restaurant.

The point is that all Jews have some way of dealing with the issue of *kosher* and nearly every aspect of Jewish life. Your Jewish neighbor surely has his own understanding of the issues of Jewish life. If you are friends with him (or her), you might inquire about these issues. It's possible to even point out some of the inconsistencies in practices as compared with the biblical teachings.

Just as the history of the Jews is intertwined with the theology of the Jews, both are intertwined with the rich and fascinating culture of the Jewish people, which we will now examine.

— 11 —

JEWISH CULTURE

— or —

Celebrating, Jewish Style

No nation, other than the Jews, was ever formed with the express purpose of being a continual testimony to the existence of God. No other people were gathered together to teach the truths of the Almighty. No other people were created to receive his words, inscribed upon tablets of stone. Because of this uniqueness, the history, religion, and culture of the Jewish people have been and always will be intertwined.

Despite this singleness of purpose, however, God has allowed for a great deal of diversity among the Jewish people. As someone has said, when you get four Jews together to discuss a matter, you will invariably end up with five opinions!

To begin with, Jews trace their cultural origins to two major groups, the *Ashkenazim* and *S'fardim*. *Ashkenazi* Jews are from the Eastern European nations and tend to be fairer-skinned. *S'fardic* Jews hail from the Mediterranean countries and are darker. The black, curly hair, and dark soulful eyes of the Israeli is a picture of the *S'fardic* Jew.

Each of the two major groups, *Ashkenazim* and *S'fardim*, has its own traditions and customs. To understand your Jewish neighbor better, ask questions about his or her background.

Additional diversity can be seen in politics. Traditionally, Jews in America have tended toward a socially liberal philosophy and consequent membership in the Democratic party. Through the years, the Democratic party seemed most sensitive to the needs of immigrants and more interested in offering aid to the downtrodden. There still is a leaning toward the left, although as Jews have become more established, they have slowly begun drifting toward a more conservative point of view.

Regarding Israel, you will also find a variety of views. Some American Jews are critical of the ways of the Israelis. Others hold fast to an "Israel, right or wrong" position. But one thing the vast majority of Jews agree on is the need for keeping Israel strong. The fact is, it was only a little more than a generation ago when Hitler led a civilized nation to exterminate 6,000,000 Jews. That vivid memory keeps Jewish people acutely aware of how important a homeland is, one in which they would be willing to make their last stand if necessary.

You may not agree with the politics of Israel, or the way things are done there, but, as a Bible-believer, you must speak to your Jewish neighbor about Israel in a non-critical, supportive way. Just as people bristle when they hear others speak badly of their mothers, Jews don't like to hear Gentiles speak badly about their motherland. Jewish people may vary when it comes to ethnic background or political views, but on the subject of Israel's survival, you will find Jews strongly united.

At the risk of sounding redundant, there is something else all Jewish people have shared: *persecution*. From Abraham onward, Jews have had to struggle to survive. Modern history has found Jews forced to live in ghettos set apart specifically for Jews. In Eastern Europe these little towns were called *shtetls*. Jews knew that safety could be found only within the environs of the *shtetl*. Outside of the village lay danger. It was easy to divide the world into two categories: "us" and "them."

This "us/them" mentality can make it hard for Jews to trust "outsiders." The truth is, many Jews, deep within, still have a basic fear of outside people. This makes your witness harder. You are most likely going to be perceived as one of "them," an outsider. Remember our chapter on credibility: identification is a key factor. It will help your witness if you can learn and appreciate the culture of your Jewish neighbor.

Appreciating Jewish food, humor, music, and other aspects of culture should not be a tough assignment. You will most likely enjoy and appreciate some of the things that make us "us." One thing is for certain, Jewish people love to celebrate.

Bar Mitzvah and *Bat Mitzvah*

When a young churchgoer is confirmed, the event is often celebrated with cookies, cakes, coffee, and punch in the church social hall following the service. Contrast this with the Jewish "confirmation" known as a *Bar* or *Bat Mitzvah,* which mean "Son" or "Daughter of the Commandment."

The typical *Bar* or *Bat Mitzvah* is held in a synagogue service on the Sabbath (Saturday) morning closest to the thirteenth birthday, although girls can become *Bat Mitzvah* anytime in their twelfth year. (I guess the rabbis consider girls to mature at a younger age than boys.) The child is actually treated as an adult and asked to participate in the regular service.

This is part of the legal rite of passage for a thirteen-year-old boy (or twelve-year-old girl). Standing before the synagogue, he or she is asked to perform adult roles in the service—reading from the *Tanakh*; chanting the blessings; giving a little *drash*, a short sermon.

The service is generally longer than your average church service, but I think you'll find it fascinating. Remember, Yeshua went to synagogue; there were no churches in his day.

After the ceremony, there is an elaborate *kiddush*, a spread of food, provided by the parents, that you wouldn't want to miss. If you are ever invited, definitely go. Not only would you be showing your support for your friend's culture and Jewishness, but you'll be treating yourself to a great time.

In recent years, the *Bar* and *Bat Mitzvah* have become more than rites of passage. They have become occasions for gala celebrations. Jewish history, fraught with catastrophe and turmoil, has caused Jewish people to look forward to such joyous occasions.

Today the *Bar* or *Bat Mitzvah* party is a first-class catered event to which relatives from far and near are invited. Beginning in the evening, eating, drinking, dancing, and general revelry carry on nonstop until the early hours of the morning.

It usually costs a great deal, so often only family and close friends are invited. If you're ever invited to a *Bar* or *Bat Mitzvah*, consider it a great honor and, by all means, go. You may not drink alcoholic beverages or believe in dancing—there will likely be both at this bash—but your not going might offend your Jewish friend.

You should also bring a nice gift. Often guests give the *Bar Mitzvah* boy or *Bat Mitzvah* girl a check. Since eighteen is the number that represents "life" in Hebrew, an eighteen-dollar check should be the minimum. That's a way of wishing long life to the young person.

The *Bar Mitzvah* is just one example of how Jewish culture differs from "Christian" culture and how Jewish history and religion have impacted it. You will probably become aware of these cultural differences as you get to know your Jewish neighbor.

Family and Education

Family has traditionally been a high priority among the Jews. In the *Torah* we find some instruction that has elevated the importance of family and education. The Lord told the Jewish people, "Honor your father and your mother, so that you may live long in the land which *Adonai* your God is giving you" (Exodus 20:12).

He also instructed Israel to "teach them [his laws] carefully to your children. You are to talk about them when you sit at home, when you are traveling on the road, when you lie down and when you get up" (Deuteronomy 6:7).

This emphasis on family and education has kept the Jewish people relatively exempt from the temptations of the world, until recently.

Today, not unlike what is going on in the rest of the world, more and more Jewish couples are getting divorced and Jewish teenagers are as susceptible to drugs as any other kids. You may find that your faith can be a beacon to draw your Jewish neighbor back to the biblical values that are at the heart and core of his own culture.

A few other cultural aspects of Jewish life find their roots in the religion of the Jewish people.

Kashrut

Kashrut refers to all the dietary laws, whereas *kosher* means "in alignment with religious law," or as I said in the last chapter, "acceptable" to God. Another way to translate it is "proper and fit." Many things can be considered *kosher*—a *Torah*, an action, a prayer shawl. But when you hear about it, you're probably thinking about food, for that is its most common application.

There are many laws of *kashrut:* how an animal should be killed, how an animal should be cooked, what animals are considered "fit" for food. The laws God gave to the Jews were to set them apart as a holy people. He didn't want his chosen ones mixing in with the pagans and their practices. The dietary laws did much to distinguish the Jews from the non-Jews, and thus kept his people unique.

Although there are many specific biblical commands concerning *kashrut*, many additional traditions developed surrounding them. To give you an example of how the *Talmud* and traditions have worked, let's look at one *kosher* law.

Deuteronomy 14:21c reads, "You are not to boil a young animal in its mother's milk." God didn't want his people boiling baby goats in their own mother's milk, possibly because it was a pagan practice, possibly to show kindness to animals. From this commandment, religious Jews have ended up with two sets of dishes for meals—one for meat products, one for milk or dairy products, and sometimes even two refrigerators, one for meat, the other for dairy.

It was this same zealous line of religious thought that led the rabbis to state that a separate set of dishes was needed exclusively for Passover. This was to ensure that there be no chance of eating leavened bread during the Passover week (the Feast of Unleavened Bread). It is *unkosher* to do so.

This all might sound a little much, and perhaps it is somewhat excessive, but the initial idea to put a "fence around the Law" was a plan to make it harder to break God's commandments. The fence was composed of tradition. Tradition became such a strong force in the life of the Jewish community that we hear the character Tevye, in *Fiddler on the Roof*, offer it as the reason Jewish people were able to keep their balance. "Without tradition," he explains, "our lives would be as shaky as a fiddler on the roof!"

Your Jewish friend may or may not keep *kosher*. He or she might keep biblically *kosher*. He or she might keep traditionally *kosher*. At home the laws of *kashrut* might be kept. In a restaurant they might be suspended. Some Jews won't eat pork, but use only one set of dishes. Others might keep all leaven out of their homes during Passover, but order shrimp if they go out to dinner.

As with other ways of my Jewish people, there are a lot of varieties on the *kosher* theme. Taking time to talk to your Jewish neighbor about his or her ideas concerning *kashrut* is the best way to gain understanding.

Circumcision

Another cultural event that finds its roots in Scripture is the ceremony that surrounds a *birth*. All of us celebrate the birth of a newborn baby. It is one of the most exquisite events in life. Jewish people have a unique ceremony surrounding the birth of a baby boy, called *B'rit Milah*, the Covenant of Circumcision. It is at this ceremony that the baby is named.

This practice goes back to the days of Abraham. Circumcision was to be a sign of the covenant God made with the Jewish people and was to be performed on each male when he was eight days old (Genesis 17:10–14).

Luke 2:21 records Yeshua's circumcision and naming:

> On the eighth day, when it was time for his *b'rit-milah*, he was given the name Yeshua, which is what the angel had called him before his conception.

I realize there is some debate today concerning the subject of circumcision. Is it good for Gentiles to circumcise their sons? Should believers, Jewish or Gentile, circumcise their sons, given Paul's thoughts on the subject expressed in Galatians? Is it an old-fashioned ceremony that should be avoided because it might be traumatic for the infant? Obviously, addressing this question is beyond the scope of this book.

For our purposes you only need to be aware that at the birth of a son and the circumcision and naming that follow, a major event is taking place. Congratulate the parents that their son has been given the sign of the covenant God made with the Jewish people, and to those who allied themselves with Israel.

Naming

The naming ceremony has variations. In Bible times, a baby boy or girl was named "So-and-so, son" or "daughter of so-and-so." This is seen where Yeshua called his disciple *Shim'on bar Yonah*, meaning *Simon son of Jonah*. There were no last names as we have today. Boys and girls were identified with their parents this way. These Hebrew names are used, even in a modern synagogue service, when calling someone to *bimah* (pulpit) to read from the *Torah*.

The Jewish people you're likely to meet will not be known by their Hebrew names. Since Jews have lived in the lands of others since the Dispersion, they have adopted names popular in the lands in which they live.

When I was born, my parents named me *Barry*, an Anglo-Saxon name. The name I was given at my circumcision, *Baruch,* Hebrew for "blessed," is rarely used. Only a few of my closest family and friends ever call me this. In America I am Barry Rubin. But if I were to live in Israel, I'd be *Baruch ben Israel*. (My father's Hebrew name was Israel.)

My Hebrew name means "Blessed son of Israel." Nice, huh! (*Ben* is Hebrew for son, whereas *bar* is Aramaic. Often these two ancient languages of the Jewish people are used interchangeably. You can see examples of this in the New Covenant.)

I, like most *Ashkenazim,* was named after a deceased relative. This tradition was developed to memorialize the dead through the living. This is another naming custom of my people.

Knowing about these auspicious occasions, the birth, circumcision, and naming of a Jewish child, will give you an opportunity to converse in an intelligent way. You could inquire about the name and what it means. You can ask about the deceased person who is being memorialized. You can even send a card or gift. It is one of those times when you can really show your love and friendship.

The Wedding

Another event in the life of your Jewish friend that is especially meaningful is a wedding. Even though Jewish weddings have similarities to Christian weddings, there are a few differences of which you should be aware. If you go to your Jewish friend's wedding or the wedding of his or her child, you may see some unusual ceremonies.

To begin with, often the parents of *both* the bride and groom walk their respective children down the aisle. By doing so they symbolize the concept of both man and woman leaving their fathers and mothers to join their mates. This is the same symbolism in a Christian wedding, except usually it's only the father who walks his daughter down the aisle.

You will see the two who are getting married standing under a canopy, called a *chupah*, which symbolizes the consummation of marriage. In biblical times, a man brought a woman into his tent and consummated their relationship. Then they were considered married. Since tents often symbolize God's covering of his people, I see the *chupah* as standing for God's covering of the union. When I conduct a wedding, this is something I mention.

Once the couple is under the canopy, the rabbi will ask the groom to repeat the following: "Be sanctified [set apart] to me with this ring in accordance with the Law of Moses and Israel." You may also hear the reading of the *k'tuvah*, or marriage contract. This, written prior to the ceremony, is the promise made by the groom to love and care for his wife, and for the wife to honor and care for her husband. The *Sheva B'rakhot,* the Seven Benedictions, are usually chanted in Hebrew by the cantor or rabbi at the close of the wedding ceremony.

At the culmination of the ceremony, it is customary to place a small glass on the floor for the groom to step on and break. The breaking of the glass has several traditional derivations, but the most prevalent one is that it commemorates the destruction of the Temple in 70 C.E. Those who understand the meaning are reminded that Judaism is incomplete without the Temple. We Jewish believers in Yeshua see that the sacrificial system was fulfilled in the atoning work of the Messiah.

Then comes the party. Since a wedding is a *simchah*, a celebration, it behooves guests to have fun. So, if you are attending a Jewish wedding, enjoy yourself! Eat, sing, dance as long as you don't have a conviction against it (and you're not on a diet). Remember, Paul said to the Jews he became as a Jew. So enjoy!

At the birth of a baby, at a *Bar* or *Bat Mitzvah*, at the marriage of a couple, you have a wonderful opportunity to grow closer to your Jewish neighbor. These occasions give you a chance to show your identification and concern for your Jewish friend. But there is no time in which to draw closer than following the death of your neighbor's loved one.

Death

To a believer, death means "absent from the body, present with the Lord." We miss the one who died but have the assurance that he or she is in a far better place. For Jewish people who don't believe, death is desperately depressing. Jewish funerals are sad affairs. Jewish people today are without a real hope of an afterlife. So, questions about the futility of life flood the mind. Some Jewish people hold a somewhat superstitious view of life beyond death, but it seems to me that most consider death the end, not the beginning.

The first seven-day period after the burial of a relative (burials are to take place as soon after death as possible, no later than three days after) is called *shiva*, which literally means "seven." During this time the family will wear an item of torn clothing. In Bible times, when people mourned they would rend, or tear, their garments. Mourners sit on low stools or boxes, not normal-sized chairs. Some actually sit on the floor. This sitting for seven days is where the expression "sitting *shiva*" comes from. No leather shoes are worn. Shaving or hair-cutting is not permitted; nor is the use of cosmetics. None of the usual pleasures of life is to be enjoyed.

It is customary during this period to visit the mourning family in the home where they are sitting *shiva*. However, since words cannot adequately express the grief the mourner is feeling, visitors are generally asked not to say anything to those mourning unless spoken to. It is also customary to allow fond discussion of the deceased if the mourner mentions the one who died. This aids the mourner through this difficult period.

Two other periods of mourning, one lasting for thirty days following the date of death, the other until the one-year anniversary, complete the mourning period.

If you are close enough to your Jewish friend, you can visit the *shiva* house. Be with your Jewish friend, letting him or her talk about the loss just experienced. It would not be in good taste to talk about the afterlife at this time, no matter what is being said. This is a time simply to recognize the sovereignty of God and emphasize God's mercy and compassion. It is not a time to discuss judgment, atonement, salvation, heaven, or hell. Your ministry to your Jewish friend should be one of comfort and consolation. Pray that the Comforter can give you words to console your Jewish neighbor.

Understanding the cultural uniqueness of your Jewish friend will go a long way toward introducing him or her to the Messiah. You will not only understand your audience, but you will grow closer as friends. It is important that you build a relationship of trust, confidence, and friendship with the person with whom you want to share. Leave the pulpit-pounding to others. You need to be a friend, ready, willing, and able to love your Jewish neighbor. The glossary in the back of the book offers you more information about the history, religion, and culture of the Jewish people that may be helpful to you in your witness.

SECTION IV

The Feedback: Barriers to Belief

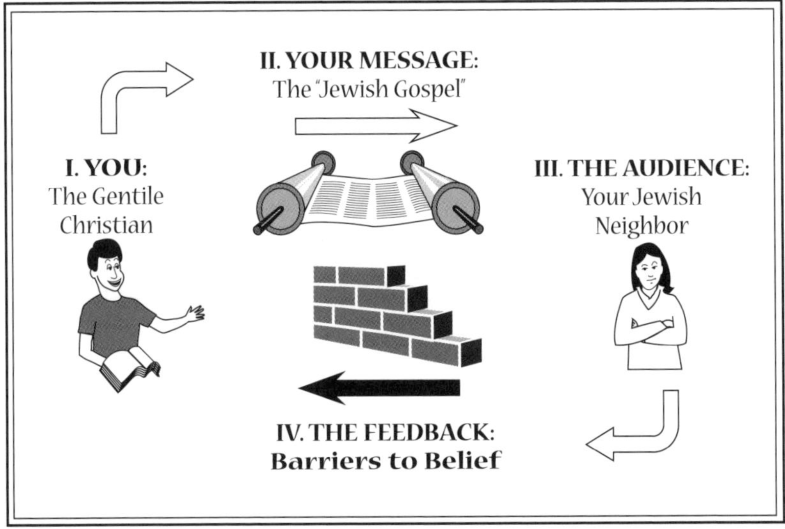

Once I watched two Jewish men debate the Messiahship of Yeshua. One was a believer, the other was not. On the surface such debates sound worthwhile, but argumentation often leads to anger, which is what happened in this case.

Assessing the impact of the debate (and there have been many such debates in history), I concluded that nothing was accomplished. Nothing, that is, except to show two Jews fighting one another.

I recount that story to you because in this section we are going to discuss barriers to belief. Although you might feel equipped to win debates, let me offer you a suggestion.

One of the traps we fall into is to suppose that all we must do is present a clear case for the Messiah and people will believe. Unfortunately, this is not true. Scripture teaches us that God's Spirit is responsible for drawing individuals to the Messiah. Faith is a gift from God.

You might ask, then, "How do I begin sharing my faith?" The answer is easy, *Clear away the clumps*. The following illustration will help you understand.

Several years ago I tried my hand at gardening. I knew next to nothing about it, but I asked around, read a little, and set out to see if my thumb was green. It wasn't! But I learned some valuable lessons in the process.

I learned about clump-clearing. The soil in which I was attempting to garden was one big lump of clay, hard as a rock. All the books I read on the subject told me that the soil had to be broken up, that clumps had to be cleared out. I spent hours and hours chopping away at those large chunks. It almost broke my back!

Later, I noticed that the seeds I had planted in the areas I prepared most diligently grew. The ones I had put in soil less rigorously primed hardly grew at all. The seeds contained within them the potential for life. My part in the process had been to encourage that life to grow.

This section is about clump-clearing—breaking up the barriers to belief. Your Jewish neighbor may be a seed waiting to germinate. By learning how to break up the barriers to belief, you can encourage the seed to grow. It is the work of God's Spirit to draw the person to the Lord. Your job is simply to start breaking up the ground and clearing out the clumps. Your Jewish neighbor might just be part of the remnant.

You will see from the witnessing model at the beginning of this section that we have arrived at the final point in the communication process. It's called Feedback, Barriers to Belief. You already have a good sense of who you are and how you may be perceived. We have discussed what the "Jewish Gospel" is all about, and you have a better idea what your Jewish neighbor is likely to believe, think, and feel.

Section IV: Feedback

You saw in Section III that the history, religion and culture of the Jewish people are intertwined. In this section, I separate them so I can teach you about the barriers to belief and how to break up these clumps so the Good News can be planted. However, we must first look at the subject of discernment.

— 12 —

THE ART OF DISCERNMENT

— or —

When is a Question Not a Question? (That is the Question)

When Yeshua sent out the twelve disciples he instructed them saying: "Pay attention! I am sending you out like sheep among wolves, so be as prudent as snakes and as harmless as doves" (Matthew 10:16). He was warning his disciples to be alert when they went out as his representatives. He wasn't calling his own Jewish people "wolves." Remember he was a Jew and was speaking to Jews, as well as about some of them. He just knew they'd face some big "challenges."

You need not be worried that your Jewish neighbor is a wolf whom you should fear. You won't face the same danger as the disciples did. Most Jewish people are kind and thoughtful. Nevertheless, Yeshua's advice is worth heeding. Be prudent as serpents and harmless as doves. Among other things, this means that you should be discerning in your witness, especially when it comes to answering questions.

There are many different kinds of questions. Some are asked to gain information. Others have different intentions.

Have you ever listened to a call-in radio show on which an expert was available to answer questions? You've probably noticed how many of the questions asked aren't really questions at all. Sometimes they appear as questions but are really statements. Sometimes they are challenges disguised as questions. Sometimes they are asked only so a person can hear himself talk.

When I first began teaching in a college I didn't have much discernment. Often students would raise their hands, ostensibly to ask a question or receive clarification. After listening for a while, I would offer what I considered to be an appropriate answer, only to find out that the question was not a question at all.

The more experience I had, the more I realized that occasionally a questioner would use his or her question time to give a little speech. The longer I taught, the more adept I became at distinguishing true questions from false questions. I developed a little discernment.

Likewise, talking with people about the Messiah requires some degree of discernment. Occasionally, a question may be raised for the purpose of challenging what you say. Sometimes a question might simply be a way of expressing personal feelings. Experience, coupled with prayer for discernment, will help you sense the question that often lies behind the question.

One characteristic of the communication style of Jewish people is to answer one question with another. For instance:

> "So, Bernie, how's your daughter?"
> "How do you think she is with five kids?"

Was Bernie asking a question? No, he's complaining on behalf of his daughter, maybe for himself, as well. Here's another example.

> "Dad, do you think you could get me a new car?"
> "A new car? Do I look like I'm made of money?"

Both of these responses to the questions appear like questions but are really answers disguised as questions. When, where, or how this style of communicating began is hard to say. But does it exist among the Jewish people? Would I lie about such a thing?

No matter when it began, a similar system was already in place at the time of Yeshua. He also answered questions with questions. You will see this as we go through this chapter.

In order for you to be more effective in communicating the Good News that Messiah has come, here are a few examples of Yeshua's communication style. They show you how he answered a question with a question—and how he applied principles of discernment.

The Challenging Question (Read Matthew 21:23–27)

The chief priests and elders of the people came to Yeshua and asked him by what authority he taught. From a human point of view, they had every right to pose this question because they were responsible for the care of the people. Yeshua's authority came from the Father and obviously exceeded theirs, but he wasn't ready to reveal this to them. He wanted to avoid responding directly. He did so by answering a question with a question.

He asked the chief priests a question he knew they wouldn't want to answer. He promised that if they first answered his question, he would respond to theirs. Before responding to their challenge, he placed the chief priests in the position of having to admit that John the Immerser had received his authority from heaven. If they refused to acknowledge this, the chief priests would arouse the anger of those who believed John to be a prophet.

Yeshua wasn't trying to make trouble. He was avoiding confrontation and challenge, and facing them with the insincerity of their question. When you talk with your Jewish friend about Jewish things, you might find yourself challenged. It might help you understand what I mean if I share some of the challenging questions I have heard.

> "Who gave you the right to tell me that Yeshua is the Messiah?"
> "Do you know Hebrew?"
> "Have you been to rabbinical school?"

Are these really questions? Not really. They are challenges. It might be wise, in such cases, to avoid answering them. Proverbs 26:5 says, "Answer a fool as his folly deserves, so that he won't think he is wise." In some ways, this proverb applies. Let's examine, for a moment, some ways you might answer the challenging question.

Suppose you were able to say honestly, "Yes, I speak fluent Hebrew and have recently graduated from rabbinical school." Do you suppose that would persuade your questioner that your point of view had suddenly become more tenable? Don't assume it for a moment! His response to your impressive credentials might likely be a flippant, "Well, you certainly didn't learn very much in rabbinical school," or even, "With such a fine education, why waste your time trying to convert Jews?" Again, these responses come from real conversations.

Of course, credentials count. And yes, there will be times when a direct answer is warranted. But you'll have to seek discernment, otherwise you risk "casting pearls before swine."

Chances are you won't hear the statements above, simply because you're not a "professional missionary," just a concerned friend. But I offer these to you as examples of challenges dressed up as questions. Pray for discernment and you will begin to detect the difference between what is sincere and what is merely designed to get you off the Gospel track.

Yeshua's approach was to sidestep the challenging question by answering with another question. If your Jewish neighbor challenges you saying, "Do you speak Hebrew?" or "Have you been to rabbinical school?" try answering with a question such as, "If I did speak Hebrew or if I had been to rabbinical school, would you be more open to believing that Yeshua might be the Messiah?" It might help your Jewish friend realize that he is really just challenging your right to share your faith with him.

Again, let me reiterate that you will probably not be challenged the way workers in Jewish ministries have been. None of your Jewish neighbors is going to expect that you've been to rabbinical school or are a Hebraicist. I just want you to see that sometimes a challenging statement comes dressed up as a question and to offer you a way to deal with it.

Remember, your right to share comes from a higher authority. That you don't speak Hebrew and that you have not been to rabbinical school has nothing to do with the fact that God has revealed to you the truth of the promised Messiah. But stating so in a forthright way might not be timely to do at this point in your witness. So, be discerning like Yeshua. Consider sidestepping the challenging question.

The Trap Question
(Read Matthew 22:15–22)

Matthew tells us that the Pharisees counseled together in order to entangle or trap Yeshua. They sent out their disciples with some Herodians, the political party that supported King Herod. After complimenting Yeshua—"Rabbi, we know that you tell the truth and really teach what God's way is"—they set their trap, "So tell us your opinion: does *Torah* permit paying taxes to the Roman Emperor or not?"

They were trying to trap him into alienating himself from either the common people or the Roman rulers. Either answer would have resulted in serious repercussions. Had Yeshua admitted that it was lawful to pay tribute to Caesar, the commoners, already heavily taxed, would have muttered resentment. If, on the other hand, Yeshua had declared it unlawful, he would have been in trouble with the government.

Once again, Yeshua answered their question with one of his own: Taking a denarius, "he asked them 'Whose name and picture are these?'" The answer was obvious: "Caesar's." He concluded, "give the Emperor what belongs to the Emperor. And give to God what belongs to God!" He never really said whether or not it was lawful. He reflected reality back to his questioners and gave no offense to either group.

Your Jewish neighbor might ask, "Do you support Israel?" This can be as loaded a question as the one posed to Yeshua centuries ago. Your Jewish neighbor knows that things are not perfect in the Land, but there may be another issue behind your neighbor's question that goes beyond current events. It is the issue of whether or not you can be trusted. Are you a friend of the Jewish people, or not? Are you an "us" or a "them"?

Israel is the Jewish homeland. In the back of the minds of many Jews is the notion that someday they might choose (or be forced) to live there. Your answer to your neighbor's question, "Do you support Israel?" will reveal a lot about you and about the faith that you are espousing. Are you to be considered trustworthy (remember our discussion on credibility)? Is what you're sharing about Yeshua safe to listen to?

Most believers I know support Israel because of what the Bible says. Not only must Jews be living in the Land before the return of the Messiah, but God guaranteed it to be a homeland for his people. Most believers would answer, "Yes, I support Israel."

There are, however, American Jews who find themselves on the horns of a dilemma. Some are embarrassed and concerned by the recurring Palestinian problem. They don't want Israel to be or appear to be violent. Yet they understand the need for a homeland.

Others support a strong stand concerning the unrest on the West Bank. Some would like to move all Palestinians out of the Land, period. American Jews have strong feelings on both sides of the issue about Israel. Some have expressed themselves in critical terms. Others are more supportive. What you need to remember is that it's the *Jewish* homeland that *Jews* are arguing about. In many ways its a family matter.

Your answer to the question, "Do you support Israel?" will require discernment. Instead of offering a quick yes or no, why not use this opportunity to clarify your position? You can present the biblical view that God promised the Land to the Jewish people (Genesis 13:14–15; 15:18–21; 26:1–5; 28:1–4). Explain that you are looking for the day when there will be lasting peace in the Land—the day when the Messiah returns to set up his kingdom of peace. You can express some thoughts about how sad you are to see young Palestinian and Jewish children hurt.

Do not feel trapped into giving a quick yes or no when more explanation is needed. For you to be critical about Israel means speaking against the "homeland." Be careful if you choose to do it.

It might not be the intention of your Jewish neighbor to trap you as the Pharisees tried to ensnare Yeshua. Still, the question might be unintentionally loaded. By avoiding an unequivocal yes or no, you may effectively use the opportunity to explain the real answer—that peace will not come until Yeshua does. Your witness will be stronger for it.

The False Question
(Read Matthew 22:23–33)

Matthew tells us that later that day, after Yeshua had dealt with the Pharisees, he was visited by the Sadducees, who presented him with a false question. The subject was resurrection, something that Yeshua had taught his disciples about. But here he was faced by the Sadducees, the sect of Jews that did not believe in the resurrection.

Their question was complex and intentionally sticky. They proposed a hypothetical situation. Suppose a man were to die, and his younger brother, following the *Torah* (Deuteronomy 25:5), were to marry the dead man's wife. Then suppose this man died and his next younger brother married the wife. Then suppose this happened to all seven brothers in the family. Whose wife would the woman be in the resurrection?

It was a false question because they were inquiring about something in which they didn't believe. Perhaps they were looking for a way to discount the rest of his teaching.

When I became a believer in Yeshua, I found myself drawn to the way in which he communicated; he was like no one I had ever studied before. But coming upon this situation with the Sadducees really stumped me. Certainly Yeshua was not naive. Why, then, did he bother to answer this false question put forth by the Sadducees?

Reading over this portion of Matthew, I found my answer in verse 33: "When the crowds heard how he taught, they were astonished." It seemed to me that Yeshua's response was not so much for the sake of the taunting Sadducees, but for the sake of the multitudes who might be led astray by their false teaching.

When you're witnessing to your Jewish neighbor, you too might be asked a false question. For example, "If Hitler had believed, could he have gone to heaven?" You could respond in a straightforward manner stating exactly what you believe. Keep in mind that this may be more than a question about your theological beliefs. It may really be designed to find out how you or your "religion" feels about the persecution of Jews.

Using discernment, you could turn the question to the subject of God's judgment, righteousness, and mercy. Express your horror at what Hitler did. Find out if your neighbor lost any family in the Holocaust. You might even ask if he or she believes in heaven and hell, and if not, why the question is really being asked. To use a term from the sales world, you might "qualify" your friend for that kind of discussion.

Look behind the question in order to discern what is really going on. Perhaps your Jewish neighbor really does care about what happened to Hitler. But, more likely he's curious about your beliefs, or is looking for a way to conveniently disengage from your witness.

The truth is, the question about Hitler is absurd. Given the nature of Hitler, and the apparent unrelenting hardening of his heart, it seems beyond comprehension for him to have repented. Truly, it's a question that doesn't deserve an answer. It's like the one about how many angels can dance on the head of a pin. Proverbs 26:4 states, "Don't answer a fool in terms of his folly, or you will be descending to his level."

In Yeshua's response to the false question posed to him, he used the opportunity to preach a little sermon on the resurrection to those within earshot. He gave an answer, but it wasn't the one that the Sadducees had expected. You, too, can use a false question to lead someone closer to the Kingdom of Heaven.

The Testing Question (Read Matthew 22:34–40 and Mark 12:28–34)

The Pharisees had sent the Herodians to Yeshua. Then the Sadducees had a go at him. Next came the Scribes, experts in the fine points of Jewish Law. Matthew tells us that their purpose was to test him.

The Scribes were technically conversant in all 613 *mitzvot* (commandments) found in the *Torah*. The study of these *mitzvot* occupied each of their waking moments. Perhaps they could get Yeshua to answer a question about these God-given standards of behavior. "Rabbi, which of the *mitzvot* in the *Torah* is the most important?"

Perhaps this was the standard test the Scribes administered to any professed teacher of the Jewish people. Or perhaps they were setting Yeshua up to give a "wrong" answer.

The logical choice for Yeshua might have been to focus upon the Sabbath, since the keeping of the Sabbath had taken on supreme importance among the Jews of that day. The rules and regulations of Sabbath-keeping had become a favorite topic of discussion. Matthew had already described a conflict that had flared up when Yeshua's disciples were accused of breaking the Sabbath by picking food (Matthew 12:1–8). Perhaps the Pharisees sought to test Yeshua's attitude concerning the Sabbath.

Another of the day's issues involved *kashrut*—keeping *kosher*. Jews were restricted in what they could eat. Pork and shrimp were out. Meat could not be eaten together with milk products. Hands had to be washed according to a prescribed fashion.

To this day there are those trained in *kashrut*, people who earn a living deciding on the fitness of certain products and procedures. If you examine the packages of many foods you will notice a "U" or a "K" in a circle. This means the food has been certified by a rabbi to be *kosher*. The Pharisees who tested Yeshua might have been interested in how highly he held these laws.

Perhaps they were interested in his thoughts on the issue of circumcision. This sign of the covenant was then and is still a controversial subject in the Jewish community. Did he think it was important?

Whatever lay behind the original question, Yeshua chose to respond to the test by quoting the *Sh'ma*. *Sh'ma* is Hebrew for "hear" and is the beginning word of the central creed of faith for Jewish people, recited twice in every synagogue service. Yeshua is quoted as saying this is the greatest commandment in:

> *Sh'ma Yisra'el, Adonai Eloheinu, Adonai echad* [Hear, O Israel, the Lord our God, the Lord is one], and you are to love *Adonai* your God with all your heart, with all your soul, with all your

understanding and with all your strength (Mark 12:29-31).

His audience stood there, amazed. In those two short sentences Yeshua had summarized the Law and the Prophets. Ignoring their actual question, he spoke to the heart of the question behind it, namely, "What is most important to God?" He did not get tangled up in the test. He went beyond it. Not only that, but all Jewish people agree that the *Sh'ma* is the greatest statement of their faith. So instead of getting mixed up in disputation over the Law, he affirmed the Law in a very Jewish way. And why wouldn't he? Wasn't he an observant Jew?

You might hear a testing question from your Jewish neighbor. He might ask something that, at first hearing, sounds irrelevant to your purpose of teaching him about his Messiah. But there might be a question behind the question.

One example focuses on the abundance of Christian denominations: "You say there is one Truth," this question begins. "Why then are there dozens of denominations, each advocating its own interpretation of the Bible?"

The answer to that question would involve a course in Church history. That's not my field, nor is it likely to be yours. But at the core it is really a question of whether or not anyone has the right to say there is one Truth. This is the issue that must be tackled. Regarding the question of Truth, you might point out that just because man is unable to agree on Truth it does not negate that there can be one Truth.

Just as Yeshua's answer soared beyond the Pharisees' testing questions, you too will need to resist the particulars and get down to the real issue, the Messiahship of Yeshua.

None of this is meant to suggest that you become impolite or evasive, but rather that you communicate in a style Yeshua used. He often answered questions with questions. He avoided answering directly if direct answers could be purposely misconstrued and misused. He wasn't afraid of confronting people with the insincerity of their queries when appropriate. Yeshua was a most effective communicator; he got his message across to his people.

You care about your Jewish neighbor. You want him or her to

know the joy of salvation. Be prudent as snakes and as harmless as doves. Discernment will help you know which creature to emulate and when.

Having touched upon the subject of discernment, let's turn to some actual questions you may face. Most of us who have been involved with sharing the Messiah with the Jewish people come up with the same lists of questions, the same clumps that need clearing. By presenting them here and explaining how the clumps got there in the first place, I hope to help you break through those barriers to belief.

— 13 —

HISTORICAL BARRIERS TO BELIEF

— or —

Breaking Through Questions of Doctrine

The first kind of clump creating a barrier to belief is what I call the historical barrier. This clump was thrown into the garden by some of the awful things in history pertaining to the Jewish people and Yeshua. Here are how some really sound.

"If Jesus was the Messiah, why have so many atrocities been committed in his name?"

As we have seen, Jewish people are acutely aware of the awful deeds that have been done to our people "in the name of Jesus." On a lesser scale, whether you know it or not, some of this may be happening in your own neighborhood.

Many Jewish children have been called "Christ-killers" by misguided peers. Many a Jewish family has been snubbed by neighbors who attend church on Sunday. Many Jews have been excluded from country clubs simply because they were Jewish. This behavior cannot be justified, but we can try to explain what lies behind it.

Those who have persecuted Jews or anyone else in the name of Jesus were probably not real believers. And even if a profession of faith had actually been made, it is safe to say that they were not *true* followers of Yeshua.

Many people, even today, attend church but have no personal relationship with the Lord. Some go because it is traditional. "My parents went, the neighbors go, my community expects it, so I'll go, too." This is not an uncommon attitude (an attitude that often prevails in the synagogue as well, by the way).

It is a good idea immediately to disclaim and disassociate yourself from the past persecutions of Jews when talking of faith with your Jewish neighbor. Express your sorrow that these atrocities have occurred—and your sadness that they have taken place by so-called Christians.

Be quick, too, to disassociate these evildoers from Yeshua himself. Nowhere do we find him espousing hatred for his own people. Even when he hung on the execution stake, abandoned by everyone, including his own *talmidim* (disciples), he pleaded, "Father, forgive them; they don't understand what they are doing" (Luke 23:34). He died willingly to atone for the sins of all people.

Yeshua taught love. He inspired gentleness. He practiced peace. He encouraged giving. There is no indication anywhere that he would have condoned the violence perpetrated by his so-called followers. Rather, he would have despised it.

Use the opportunity, if confronted with this question, to encourage your Jewish neighbor to read the Sermon on the Mount. It should be evident that persecution of Jews is far from what Yeshua stood for.

"How can I trust the New Testament? It's anti-Jewish, anti-Semitic!"

Your neighbor may at one time have read some of the New Covenant and come across what he might consider hateful diatribes against the Jewish people. Certain statements from the New Covenant appear to attack some of the Jewish people. In fact, some of these verses have been used to justify anti-Semitic attitudes and behavior.

How do you explain these statements?

First, remind your neighbor that the New Covenant is a Jewish document, written *about* Jews, *by* Jews and *for* Jews (and non-Jews).

We might consider their comments this way. It is not uncommon to criticize one's relatives, particularly within the context of a family gathering. "Cousin Rozzie ought to lose weight," or "It's about time Uncle Harry got a job." But let an outsider say anything about Cousin Rozzie or Uncle Harry, and they will be vigorously defended. Likewise, the New Covenant recorded some statements from Jews about other Jews. That can't be anti-Semitic.

Still, even the most avid antagonist of Yeshua might admit that the harsh things said concerning some of the Jewish people were true. Writings from the time of Yeshua point out that the criticism in the New Covenant leveled at *some* Jews was on target. But not *all* Jews.

Corruption had infiltrated the office of the high priest, so much so that it had become a political, rather than religious, office. A sense of self-righteousness prevailed among many of the Pharisees. The *am ha'aretz*, the common people, were disdained by the leadership in Israel. The Judean Jews, those around Jerusalem, looked down their noses at the Galilean Jews. In fact, many of the New Covenant references to "the Jews" are really about the Judean Jews. They had a superior attitude toward the Galilean Jews. Sin was present in the Land.

The New Covenant is not alone in pointing out these problems. The *Talmud* addressed these problems, too. But since the *B'rit Chadashah* was misused by anti-Semites through the years to persecute Jews, it is now seen as anti-Semitic.

Yeshua's criticism of the hypocritical practices of some of the Jewish people was nothing new. The accusations were no harsher than those of the ancient prophets of Israel. It was Isaiah who spoke the following:

> Oh, sinful nation, a people weighed down by iniquity, descendants of evildoers, immoral children! They have abandoned *Adonai*, spurned the Holy One of Isra'el, turned their backs on him! Isaiah 1:4

No, the words of the Newer Covenant are not anti-Jewish. Yeshua did not hate his own people. He, like the prophets before him, hated sin. The statements he made were directed at certain Jews and they concerned particular problems. His words were no harsher than many found in the "Older" Covenant. In all of Scripture, God's purpose in confronting sin was that he could show his steadfast and everlasting love when his people repented. If Yeshua was anti-Semitic, so was Isaiah.

"If Jesus is the Messiah, why haven't rabbis believed in him?"

To begin with you need to know something that may surprise you. Although you'd think that Jewish people would listen carefully to their rabbi, giving this barrier to belief some basis, the truth is that most Jews nowadays are not too concerned with what the rabbis believe or teach. There are groups in which the rabbi truly does have the last word. The members of these ultra-Orthodox groups, called *Chasidim*, submit to the authority of their rabbis. It is unlikely that your Jewish neighbor is part of one of these groups, since they generally live together in tightly knit and self-sufficient communities.

So, your Jewish neighbor might be bringing up the question about the rabbis' unbelief in Yeshua as a way of saying, "If our Jewish scholars don't buy into your conclusion that Jesus is the Messiah, then why should I?"

Your response might be that many rabbis *have* believed. Yeshua himself was called *Rabbi*. Paul, the former Saul of Tarsus, was a noted rabbi. Nicodemus, who came to Yeshua by night, was called a ruler of the Jews and was a rabbi. Through the years there have been many rabbis who have believed.

"Then why don't we know about them?" your neighbor might ask. But even as he does, he will already realize the answer to this question. If a rabbi became a believer in Yeshua, he would be immediately defrocked and his name expunged from the rabbinical records. He certainly would not receive publicity in the Jewish community. His credibility would be brought into question. Murmuring concerning his mental state or his commitment to the Jewish people and to the *Torah* would be heard.

Scripture teaches that eyes of faith are a gift from God. "God has mercy on whom he wants, and he hardens whom he wants" (Romans 9:18). Yeshua preached to the lowly; his message did not appeal to those who considered themselves experts in God's ways. Paul showed his understanding of God when he wrote that "God chose what the world considers nonsense in order to shame the wise; and God chose what the world considers weak in order to shame the strong . . . so that no one should boast before God" (1 Corinthians 1:27, 29).

"We Jews have never proselytized. Why don't you just leave us alone?"

To begin with, it is *not* historically true that Jews have never proselytized. Today, it might be said that Jews don't proselytize, but centuries ago it was not that way.

The very reason God chose Israel was to be a light unto the nations, the Gentiles. Throughout Bible history, the Jews are seen as a testimony people, from the Tabernacle to the Messiah. It was always God's intention to use this people to bring glory to himself and show the world a better way. Moses expressed it this way:

> Look, I have taught you laws and rulings, just as *Adonai* my God ordered me, so that you can behave accordingly in the land where you are going in order to take possession of it. Therefore, observe them; and follow them; for then all peoples will see you as having wisdom and understanding. When they hear of all these laws, they will say, "This great nation is surely a wise and understanding people." For what great nation is there that has God as close to them as *Adonai* our God is, whenever we call on him? What great nation is there that has laws and rulings as just as this entire Torah which I am setting before you today? Deuteronomy 4:5–8

Through the ages, the nation of Israel has been a testimony to the existence and love of a living God. Who could read the Scripture accounts of God's wooing his people back from sin and rebellion (the book of Hosea is a moving example) and doubt his commitment to this people? In spite of centuries of dispersion in unfriendly foreign lands and untold persecutions, who can deny that a supernatural force has been protecting the Jewish people?

In the early days of the New Covenant there was much outreach activity on the part of the Jewish people. Finding themselves dispersed throughout the Middle East, they made many converts to Judaism. References in the New Covenant to proselytes and God-fearing Gentiles indicate that the Jewish people were not averse to bringing outsiders into Judaic practices. After all, they were only doing their job, bearing the light of monotheism to the polytheistic pagan nations.

The ultimate performance of this role, of course, was by the apostle Paul, an observant Jew who became the bearer of the Good News to the Gentile world.

If we believe what Yeshua said, it behooves believers to be sharing his message with anyone we can find, as Paul said, "to the Jew especially, but equally to the Gentile" (Romans 1:16). Call it communicating. Call it proselytizing. Call it missionizing. Does it matter what it's called if the message is true? Believers are obliged to preach the Good News, and not exclude anyone, especially the Jews.

When Jewish people say, "We don't proselytize," what they are really saying is, "You shouldn't either." The implication is that there is no Truth, that one person's opinion is as good as another's. It is an admission that the Jewish people are a long way from the days of being a light to the nations. But if there *is* a truth, a real objective truth, then sharing that truth is always appropriate.

If your Jewish neighbor were dying of a disease for which you had the cure, the administration of that remedy would certainly be timely and fitting. It would not be considered proselytizing. It would be called caring.

Telling Jews about the Messiah is a far more caring thing to do even than sharing a cure for disease. Spiritual wholeness, having the relationship with God that he intended, is more important than physical well-being.

It is a sad indictment of modern-day Judaism that there is little proselytizing. Perhaps if the Jewish people were convinced of the truth of Judaism as it is observed today, they would find it to be a message compelling them to share. Regardless of this, if *you* know the truth, then you also know that the truth ought to be proclaimed, especially to those people to whom that truth was first revealed.

The statement that "Jews don't proselytize" is merely a modern-day phenomenon, for in the past Jews fulfilled their role as a testimony people. Further, you ought to make it very clear that you are not witnessing so as to "convert" your Jewish neighbor and turn him or her into a Gentile; your only interest is to help your Jewish neighbor meet the Messiah. You have the cure for much more than disease; you have the cure for sin.

Don't be ashamed of your efforts to share. It may cause some friction, but if you have laid the foundation for your relationship, that friendship will withstand this new dimension.

Remember, most of the historical barriers to belief are built upon misunderstanding. If you take the time to talk with and listen to your Jewish neighbor, you might be able to break up some of these barriers, clearing out the clumps to prepare the soil for planting.

— 14 —

THEOLOGICAL BARRIERS TO BELIEF

— or —

Breaking Through Two Thousand Years of Confusion

There are some barriers to belief that we could classify as theological clumps. They, like historical barriers, have to be broken up so that the Good News can germinate. These barriers, too, are often put in the form of questions.

"How can you Christians worship three gods? We Jews worship one!"

This misconception is common among Jewish people who don't understand what is meant by the Trinity (or tri-unity). I remember thinking that the Trinity was a kind of holy family: God, the holy Father; the virgin Mary, the holy Mother; and Jesus Christ, the holy Son.

But even when Jewish people understand that the Trinity is really Father, Son and Holy Spirit, it still sounds suspiciously like three gods. And if this is true, it is tantamount to polytheism, a non-biblical belief, anathema to Jews.

A word of friendly advice. Don't fall into the trap of trying to explain the doctrine of the Trinity. If God wanted us to have an easy explanation, he would have provided us with one! Theologians have wrestled with ways to explain the unique nature of God for years.

There are explanations such as the triune nature of water—liquid, ice, and steam. But that and other explanations really seem to fall short. Nothing on this earth is wholly satisfactory to explain the unique nature of the creator of the universe. It would be arrogant for us to assume the task of trying to explain his nature, beyond that which he has carefully revealed.

But there is an answer to the accusation "You Christians worship three gods." Reply simply, "No, we don't!" As mentioned in the introduction to this section, Yeshua himself, quoting the *Sh'ma* (Deuteronomy 6:4), said, "Hear, O Isra'el, the LORD our God, the LORD is one" (Mark 12:29). Yeshua espoused monotheism!

You can also show that the word translated "one" in the *Sh'ma* is the Hebrew word *echad*. *Echad* is a word that indicates a composite unity, as in Adam and Eve becoming "one flesh" (Genesis 2:24). There is another Hebrew word, *yachid*, which is also translated "one," indicating an absolute singular unity, like the number one. But in the *Sh'ma*, the central creed of Jewish faith, the Spirit moved upon Moses in such a way that he chose to write the word *echad*.

So sensitive was this issue that the great rabbi and scholar Maimonides, in his "Thirteen Articles of Faith," took great pains to substitute the word *yachid* for *echad* in his description of God's nature, even to the point of rephrasing the *Sh'ma*. Many feel that this was his attempt to counter the Trinitarian view espoused by the Church. Nonetheless, what Maimonides did was contrary to the *Tanakh* since nowhere does it refer to God as *Adonai Yachid*.

You could also show some allowance in the *Tanakh* for the concept of composite unity. For instance, the Hebrew Scriptures frequently use plural references for God. The Hebrew word *Elohim*, translated "God," is plural. This is not a great argument, however, because there are some other plausible explanations for using this plural form.

You might also point to some ancient Jewish writings that refer to a "threefold divine manifestation" of God. But it is probable that neither you nor your neighbor has ever curled up with the *Zohar*, a book of Jewish mystical writings, to read about these emanations of the god-head.

The simplest way for you to respond to the question of the Trinity, and the ground on which you might feel most comfortable, would be simply to say, "I know why you think that, but really we believers don't worship three gods at all. In fact, we worship the God of Israel—the God of Abraham, Isaac, and Jacob—the same God you worship."

There are some specific Bible references that support the plural unity of God. Isaiah 48:16 reads,

> Come close to me, and listen to this: since the beginning I have not spoken in secret, since the time things began to be, I have been there; and now *Adonai* Elohim has sent me and his Spirit.

This passage—in which God was speaking through the prophet Isaiah—seems to involve three divine persons: the "Sovereign Lord," "me," and "his Spirit." The "me" spoken of seems to have the same eternal nature as God himself, yet is sent by God, along with his Spirit.

There are also references to "the angel of the Lord," who is identified with God. In Genesis 16:7–12, "the angel of *Adonai*" spoke to Hagar, Sarai's handmaid. Genesis 16:13 states, "So she named *Adonai* who had spoken with her El Ro'i [God of seeing]." A similar scene is in Genesis 22, where "the angel of *Adonai*" constrained Abraham from slaying his son. These verses clearly identify "the angel of *Adonai*" with God.

There are references to the Holy Spirit, or the Spirit of God, as far back as Genesis 1:2: "the Spirit of God hovered over the surface of the water." Isaiah 11:2 says, "the Spirit of *Adonai* will rest on him" (the Messiah). There are many other examples as well where "the Spirit of God" performs many of the activities and functions attributed to God.

One last comment on this subject. Occasionally you will hear the related statement, "How can God have a son?" Granted, the concept of Yeshua's sonship is a little hard to grasp. Obviously, Yeshua was not a son in the way in which we are familiar with the term. He wasn't born from God's wife as you might find in Greek mythology. He didn't "grow up in God's home" as our sons do in ours. His sonship means something entirely different. Let me explain what I mean.

To use the word *son* expresses the idea that one possesses the specific personality and identity of the father. This does not always mean solely a physical bond. For instance, Yeshua renamed James and John *Boanerges,* "Sons of Thunder," giving us a vivid picture of two boisterous men who deserved this fitting nickname (Mark 3:17).

Early in Israel's history God spoke of Israel as "my firstborn son" (Exodus 4:22).

In one way we all can be considered sons of God. But Yeshua was different. He was *the* Son of God. He was God's unique Son, the perfect one, because he was the incarnation of God himself.

According to Hebrews 1:3, "This Son is the radiance of the *Sh'khinah*, the very expression of God's essence." Like the rays from the sun, Yeshua shows us the true essence of all that is God. Sun rays are not the sun itself, but they are inseparable from it, because without the sun, there would be no rays. Yet we know the rays are distinct because we can see the light in the sky of suns of other solar systems that have long since burned out. What we see are the rays that were generated by those suns thousands of years ago.

Two other passages support the truth that God has a Son. Psalm 2:7 states: "You are my son; today I became your Father." This psalm was applied by Luke at Acts 13:33. Also see Matthew 3:17.

A second and perhaps even more persuasive passage comes in the form of a riddle from the *Tanakh* and can even be used that way in your own sharing. It asks:

> Who has gone up to heaven and come down? Who has cupped the wind in the palms of his hand? Who has wrapped up the waters in his cloak? Who established all the ends of the earth? What is his name, and what is his son's name? Surely you know!
>
> Proverbs 30:4

All of the tri-unity can be found in the *Tanakh*. That in itself allows for this seemingly foreign concept to be considered "*kosher*" for Jewish people. But, once again, explaining it thoroughly is too tall an order for even the best theologian.

I suggest when sharing with your Jewish neighbor that you simply show Yeshua's teaching that God is one, seen in his quoting of the *Sh'ma*. Further, you might share some of the other verses I have offered to show that the Older Covenant allows for—and even points to—the composite nature of the one true God.

"How can a man be born from a virgin? This is simply not possible!"

Obviously your Jewish neighbor is referring to the miraculous conception of Yeshua. And, interestingly enough, the explanation to this question is one of the easier ones to offer your Jewish neighbor.

The question really goes back to the sovereignty of God. If God can create the heavens and the earth and all that is in them out of nothing, as taught in *Tanakh*, then creating a person through miraculous means is really no problem. For us it would be impossible. For God, it's no big deal.

Also, consider the fact that it was through miraculous conceptions that God created the Jewish people. It is no coincidence that the mothers of the people of the promise—Sarah, Rebekah, and Rachel—were barren. Genesis 18:11; 25:1 and 29:31 teach us that God opened the wombs of the matriarchs. Since it was through the divine and miraculous intervention of the Almighty God that the Jewish nation was born, it is entirely consistent that the redeemer of the Jewish people would also be born through miraculous means.

Couldn't it be true that in these divine acts, God was giving us a hint of the future miraculous birth by which the Messiah would come to dwell among us? Remember your Jewish friend might be operating from an anti-supernatural bias. The miraculous conception of Yeshua would really be no problem for the God who created the heavens and the earth.

"How can you believe in substitutionary atonement? We Jews don't believe that anyone can atone for someone else's sins!"

The statement that Jews don't believe in substitutionary atonement is both true and false. Nowadays, it is true. But in Bible days it would have been false.

Since the destruction of the Temple and the end of the sacrificial system in 70 C.E., rabbis have tried to offer alternative methods to atone for sin. With the loss of the Temple, the only place for the sacrifice was gone. And without the sacrifice, there was no scriptural way to atone for sin.

Discussions concerning this dilemma appear throughout Jewish writings. "How do we make the reconciliation with God that he requires without his prescribed sacrifice?" the sages asked. Instead of recognizing that God himself had fulfilled the sacrificial requirement once and for all through the death of Yeshua, the rabbis set out to find another solution.

The answer they developed centered around "works." Performing *mitzvot*, good deeds, they reasoned, must be God's alternative plan for atonement. While there is nothing wrong with performing good deeds, this was never God's plan for atonement lest people get self-satisfied.

Three particular *mitzvot* were offered as solutions for the problem of the missing Temple. First was *t'shuvah* (repentance), then *tz'dakah* (charity), and finally *t'filah* (prayer). These activities were the rabbis' alternative program for earning forgiveness. On *Yom Kippur*, the Day of Atonement, no sacrifice is offered; instead, Jewish people practice *t'shuvah, tz'dakah,* and *t'filah.*

And so, today, Jewish people report, "We Jews don't believe in substitutionary atonement!" So when you, in your Jewish Gospel message, present the fact that Yeshua died for their sins, they probably won't relate to it. The concept is foreign.

Jewish people, especially those committed to keeping other Jewish people from being exposed to the Gospel, are fond of quoting Hosea 6:6, "What I desire is mercy, not sacrifices." This is a misapplication of the verse. Some may be reacting to what is seen as hypocrisy, where a sinner comes to church on Sunday, is "absolved" of his sins, only to go out and sin again the next week. Any true believer would hardly consider this form of religion to be walking the walk of true Messianic faith.

Those who misapply Hosea 6:6 in an attempt to discount the sacrifice of Yeshua assume that the *B'rit Chadashah*, the New Covenant, doesn't teach that God desires more from his children than the motions of religion. What they fail to see is that Yeshua quotes this very verse, as seen in Matthew 9:13.

The question boils down to this: Do believers teach that all you need to have is a sacrifice and you will be saved? The answer is no! John the Immerser proclaimed, "Turn from your sins to God, for the Kingdom of Heaven is near" (Matthew 3:2). Yeshua, the Messiah, restated this same message at the beginning of his public ministry (Matthew 4:17).

James, in his discussion of faith and works, echoes this very sentiment:

> What good is it, my brothers, if someone claims to have faith but has no actions to prove it? Is such "faith" able to save him? Thus, faith by itself, unaccompanied by actions, is dead.
>
> James 2:14, 17

James says that we are saved by the kind of faith that results in good works. Otherwise, our faith is stillborn. He is not suggesting that works are required *for* salvation; he is saying that works should result *from* salvation. This is why Yeshua teaches, "You will recognize them by their fruit" (Matthew 7:20).

Believers ought to have no dispute with the desire of the Jewish people to perform *mitzvot*, good deeds. Indeed, society has prospered because of the worthwhile and noble contributions of Jewish people. *Good deeds, however, do not atone for sin.* For this, God set up a system of atonement stated in Leviticus: "For the life of a creature is in the blood, and I have given it to you on the altar to make atonement for yourselves; for it is the blood that makes atonement because of the life" (17:11).

Since most Jews are unfamiliar with the concept of vicarious or substitutionary atonement, you may find this a barrier to belief. Therefore, you'll need to show your Jewish neighbor this essential component of faith, with its foundation in Leviticus and its fulfillment in Yeshua. Isaiah 53 depicts a Jewish person dying for the sins of his people. Daniel 9 describes the Messiah as being "cut off" before the destruction of the Temple. Taken together, these passages compose a pretty good argument for what Yeshua did when he died on the Roman execution stake (cross) on a hill called Calvary.

"Why do you Christians believe in the dead coming back to life? We Jews don't believe in the resurrection of the dead."

If your neighbor argues that Jewish people don't believe in resurrection, you can contend that resurrection is indeed a Jewish concept. Not only can it be found in the *Tanakh*, but resurrection was and is taught by religious Jews to this day.

What your Jewish neighbor is really saying is, "Most Jews don't believe in the resurrection of the dead." That is true. But here are a few references to resurrection found in the *Tanakh*:

> Many of those sleeping in the dust of the earth will awaken, some to everlasting life and some to everlasting shame and abhorrence. Daniel 12:2

> Should I ransom them from the power of Sh'ol? Should I redeem them from death? Hosea 13:14

As we saw before, the Sadducees, who did not believe in resurrection, came to Yeshua ostensibly to question him about it, underscoring the fact that it was a prevalent doctrine at this time.

Maimonides, the great rabbinical scholar of the 1100s, wrote in his "Thirteen Articles of Faith," Article Thirteen:

> I believe with perfect faith in the resurrection of the dead at a time which will please the Creator, blessed be His name, and exalted be His memory for ever and ever.

This was written more than a thousand years after the time of Yeshua.

Clearly, Jews believed in resurrection in the days of *Tanakh*, in the days of Yeshua, and for hundreds, even thousands of years since. I'm quite confident that if you talk to Orthodox Jews today, you will find this belief present in their religious thinking.

One Orthodox rabbi, Pinchas Lapide, wrote that he is convinced that Yeshua himself was resurrected from the dead. On the back cover of his book, *The Resurrection of Jesus: A Jewish Perspective,* he is quoted as saying, "I accept the resurrection of Easter Sunday not as an invention of the community of disciples, but as a historical event." This man, however, is not ready to confess that Yeshua is the Messiah. Rather, he says he is the Messiah for the Gentiles.

Jews do—or at least did—believe in the resurrection of the dead. That is something you'll need to teach your Jewish friend should you hear the statement, "Jews don't believe in the resurrection of the dead."

"What makes you believe in an afterlife? We Jews don't believe in heaven or hell."

Once again this statement reveals how far popular Judaism has strayed from the once-accepted truths of biblical and Jewish theology. Although there is less emphasis on the afterlife than one finds in most Christian circles, the doctrines of heaven and hell do have strong roots in Jewish thought.

In Jewish parlance, "heaven" is *Gan Eden*, literally, "the Garden of Eden," and *ha'olam haba,* "the world to come"; hell is *Gehenna,* referencing a dump where garbage was burned.

It was said of Yochanan ben Zakai, mentioned earlier in connection with the development of rabbinic Judaism, that on his deathbed he was fearful for the future. Asked by his disciples why he was crying, he said that he didn't know which way he would go when he met his maker.

Today's most widely held position by those who *do* believe in an afterlife is usually that the quality of one's deeds determines where a person ends up. Tradition teaches that each year on *Rosh HaShanah*, the Jewish New Year, God opens up his books in heaven. These are considered to be his books of accounts, with assets and liabilities. Reviewing a person's life during the year, God prepares to write his name in one of three places: in the book of the totally righteous, in the book of totally unrighteous, or in the book of the in-between.

As you might expect, most everyone qualifies for inclusion in the book of the in-between. You are then given ten days, until *Yom Kippur*, to make amends with those whom you have wronged in the past year, to balance your account. These ten days are called the Days of Awe, *Yomim Nora'im*, and when they are over, Jewish tradition teaches that your fate is sealed for the next year.

Although heaven and hell are not widely-held doctrines, they still do exist in Jewish theology, and though most Jewish people don't believe in the system, the system is still there. If your Jewish friend says that Jews don't believe in these concepts, you can show that it may be true today, but historically it is not.

"If Jesus was the Messiah, why isn't there peace on earth?"

Today, Jewish people who are truly looking for the Messiah expect him to bring peace to the earth as is stated in Scripture:

> He will judge between the nations and arbitrate for many peoples. Then they will hammer their swords into plow-blades and their spears into pruning-knives; nations will not raise swords at each other, and they will no longer learn war.
>
> Isaiah 2:4

> The wolf will live with the lamb; the leopard lie down with the kid; calf, young lion and fattened lamb together, with a little child to lead them. Isaiah 11:6

These and other portions of Scripture that talk about world peace are associated with the coming of the Messiah. In past generations Jewish people waxed on about all the wonderful things that would happen "when the Messiah comes." There would be no more poverty, suffering, pain, and certainly no more war.

You can understand, then, that people familiar with the predictions of world peace and universal prosperity have trouble seeing in Yeshua the fulfillment of their expectations. I often hear, "There have been more wars since the time of Jesus than in all the history before him!" This is undoubtedly true. And it's a sad commentary on the supposedly enlightened world in which we live, especially a world with so many believers. This, too, however is foretold in the Word of God:

> When he [Yeshua] was sitting on the Mount of Olives, the *talmidim* [disciples] came to him privately. "Tell us," they said, "when will these things happen? And what will be the sign that you are coming, and that the *'olam hazeh* [this world/age] is ending?"
>
> Yeshua replied: "Watch out! Don't let anyone fool you! For many will come in my name, saying, 'I am the Messiah!' and they will lead many astray. You will hear the noise of wars nearby and the news of wars far off; see to it that you don't become frightened. Such things must happen, but the end is yet to come. For peoples will fight each other, nations will fight each other, and there will be famines and earthquakes in various parts of the world. Matthew 24:3-7

This is not a comforting description. But it's something we can identify around us. These words were spoken by the Messiah, not preaching peace and prosperity, but describing a world to which he would one day return. With that return he will bring the peaceful reign that Jewish people expect from the Messiah, as it is written:

> Then I saw a new heaven and a new earth, for the old heaven and the old earth had passed away, and the sea was no longer there. Also I saw the holy city, New Yerushalayim [Jerusalem], coming down out of heaven from God, prepared like a bride beautifully dressed for her husband. I heard a loud voice from the throne say, "See! God's *Sh'khinah* [the glorious manifest presence of God] is with mankind, and he will live with them. They will be his people, and he himself, God-with-them, will be their God. He will wipe away every tear from their eyes. There will no longer be any death; and there will no longer be any mourning, crying or pain; because the old order has passed away." Revelation 21:1-4

To deal with the difficulty that Messiah has come, yet did not establish world peace, you must show that his work is not finished. Yeshua told his followers that there will not only be more and more wars, but famines, earthquakes, and bad news in the world.

The good news is that there will be an end to all bad news. But you need to point out that no one enters the kingdom without establishing peace with God, as it is written; "So, since we have come to be considered righteous by God because of our trust, let us continue to have *Shalom* [peace] with God through our Lord, Yeshua the Messiah" (Romans 5:1).

Now that you are better equipped to break up the historical and theological barriers, let's turn to some of the personal barriers to belief you might face as you share the Good News with your Jewish neighbor.

— 15 —

PERSONAL BARRIERS TO BELIEF

— or —

Breaking Through Individual Objections to Faith

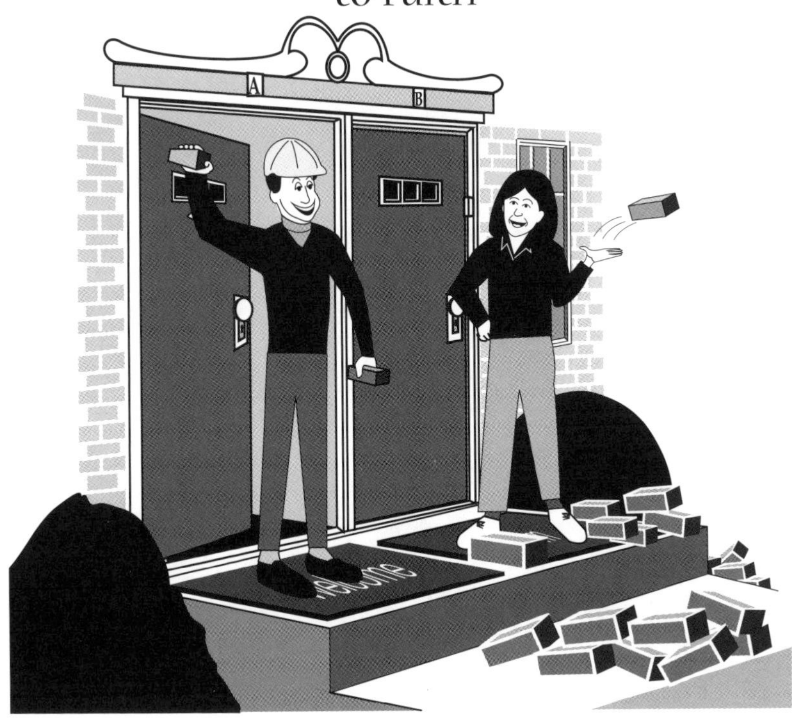

Why do I need someone to atone for my sins? I'm a good person!

This is one of the biggest personal barriers to belief there is. It's a big clump that needs to be cleared.

None of us finds it easy to face our sins. Most of us have a highly developed system of what psychologists call "defense mechanisms." Yet the Bible teaches that we all sin and come short of the glory of God.

Your Jewish neighbor may actually be one of the finest, most decent people you know. Jews are renowned for their concern for the downtrodden, care for the sick, and commitment to civil justice. They often adhere to high standards of behavior and, as a group, strive to be morally superior to others around them. Remember, the Jewish people were to set an example for the rest of the nations. Even when a Jew does not believe in God, there exists a leftover sense of responsibility to uphold high standards of moral conduct.

Assuming that your Jewish neighbor is a "good person," you need to communicate that God is not dealing merely with outward manifestations of kindness and goodness. He looks on the heart and judges sin. He knows what is going on deep down inside.

The rabbis describe two forces operating within a person: the *yetzer hatov*, the good inclination, and the *yetzer hara*, the evil inclination. They say these inclinations impact moral choice. The apostle Paul described his struggle as a continual warring between the flesh and the spirit. He summed it up in words with which we all can readily identify, "For I don't do the good I want; instead, the evil that I don't want is what I do" (Romans 7:19). In other words, even he could not live up to the high standard of God's righteousness.

Most people, although hesitant to admit that they are sinners, sense that both Paul's statement and the rabbinical concept ring loudly with truth. Man has a propensity to sin. That nature is what Yeshua came to deal with. He came to atone for our sins and, by the Spirit of God, do away with anything that goes against the will of God.

Your Jewish neighbor needs to feel assured of a few things: that you value his or her friendship; that you appreciate the good things he or she does; and that you believe God is also glad for those good deeds.

But your Jewish neighbor also needs to understand what Isaiah wrote concerning himself and his people: "All of us are like someone unclean, all our righteous deeds like menstrual rags" (Isaiah 64:6, 64:5 in Jewish Bibles). Your Jewish neighbor needs to hear what King David had to say: "No one does what is right, not a single one" (Psalm 14:3). He needs to recognize that Abraham sinned (Genesis 12:10–20); that Moses sinned (Numbers 20:7–13); that even the beloved David sinned (2 Samuel 11:1–12:12).

Your Jewish neighbor must become aware of the truth that any sin, external or internal, has its consequences; that sin is more a matter of the heart than of the hand; that there is an eternal, spiritual consequence to this sin that affects him and God.

> Rather, it is your own crimes that separate you from your God; your sins have hidden his face from you, so that he doesn't hear.
>
> Isaiah 59:2

As good as your Jewish neighbor is, surely he recognizes that he has encountered an evil inclination within him, a fleshly thought, a secret sin. In God's eyes, covert sins count as much as overt ones. He or she needs to know this.

One Saturday evening while shopping at a mall, I had an opportunity to share the message of the Messiah with some Jewish people. After I explained why the Messiah had to die, they smiled patiently and objected, "But we're good people; we don't need anyone to make atonement for us."

"Do you obey God's laws?" I asked them.

"Certainly!" came the reply.

"What did you do today?" I asked, judging from the number of bags they were carrying that they had spent a good part of the day shopping.

They answered, "We were here at the mall."

"So how is it that obeying the fourth commandment?"

They weren't sure what the fourth commandment was. I reminded them that we Jews were commanded to keep the Sabbath holy. Obviously they were not keeping it too holy there at the mall.

They became aware that they were relying on their *own* standard for goodness and righteousness. In essence, they had made up their own religion. Many Jewish people will sum up their religious conviction by saying, "I don't do anything that would hurt anyone else." At the same time, though, they don't keep the ways of God.

When he was asked what the greatest commandment was, Yeshua said it was to love God. To love God mans to obey him and seek to please him. This is where many of us fall short. Yes, we might do good things, but, too often, we fail to love God first.

My Jewish people have done their share of good things. This is great! But doing good deeds in an unbelieving context can lead to self-righteousness and turning away from God. It is the nature of humankind. And it was for this very reason that God provided a way to reconcile with him. Yeshua is that way.

"If I believe in Yeshua, I won't be Jewish anymore!"

This objection always gets to me. It shows just how far Messianic faith has gotten from its Jewish roots. The Church today feels about as Jewish as ham and cheese on white bread with mayonnaise.

What am I saying? For nineteen hundred years, most followers of Yeshua have been Gentiles with little recognition of the Jewish beginnings of their faith. But it wasn't always like this.

If you recall the debate of Acts 15, the question concerning the Jerusalem Council revolved around whether or not Gentiles could be saved without first submitting to Jewish Law, thereby becoming Jewish. Since nearly all the early believers were Jewish, they were not sure how to instruct the non-Jews who also followed the Jewish Messiah.

Certain Jews—particularly among the Pharisees who believed in Yeshua—felt "It is necessary to circumcise them and direct them to observe the *Torah* of Moshe [Moses]" (Acts 15:5). After much debate Peter stood and said,

> And God, who knows the heart, bore them witness by giving the *Ruach HaKodesh* to them, just as he did to us; that is, he made no distinction between us and them, but cleansed their heart by trust. So why are you putting God to the test now by placing a yoke on the neck of the *talmidim* which neither our fathers nor we have had the strength to bear? No, it is through the love and kindness of the Lord Yeshua that we trust and are delivered—and it's the same with them. Acts 15:8–11

Finally the Council agreed to follow James' suggestion to write the Gentiles at Antioch "to abstain from things polluted by idols, from fornication, from what is strangled and from blood" (verse 20). The letter was delivered in person by Paul and Barnabas and the community rejoiced because of its encouragement.

But in a short time, the Jewishness of Christianity greatly diminished. In relatively few years, what had started out as a Jewish sect became a Gentile religion.

Nowadays, a new Jewish believer goes through an unmistakable identity crisis. I can still remember lying on my bed the night I invited Yeshua into my life. I was afraid to go to sleep for fear that I might awaken as a Gentile. It wasn't that I was anti-Gentile. Some of my best friends were Gentiles. I just felt determined to maintain my Jewish identity. For the first time in my life, I understood that God had a special plan for the Jewish people. He had made me a Jew. Still, that night I was fearful that belief in Yeshua might put pressure on me to abandon my heritage. After all, most believers I had met *were* Gentiles.

But the next morning I awoke craving a bagel, lox, and cream cheese sandwich. Boy, was I relieved!!!

Actually, I knew in my head I was still a Jew and that nothing would ever change that fact. Believing in Yeshua might have made me an unusual Jew, but a Jew, nonetheless. Being Jewish is a matter of birth, not choice (except for those who convert to Judaism). I was born a Jew and I'll die a Jew. But thanks to God, when I die as a Jew, I will be in heaven because of the work of another Jew, Yeshua of Nazareth.

If your Jewish neighbor wonders whether or not he will remain a Jew after accepting Yeshua, assure him that he will. There have been other Jews claiming to be the Messiah. They all had their followers. Bar Kokhba, the hero who died in the Roman revolt, had many. Did his devotees cease to be Jews because they followed him? Of course not. And no rabbi today believes Bar Kokhba was the Messiah.

Shabbetai Zvi proclaimed himself to be the Messiah in the 1600s. He had quite a following in Europe. But when he ran into some trouble he converted to Islam. Obviously, he was not the Messiah. But his Jewish followers remained Jewish.

Others who made Messianic claims had followers who believed they were the Messiah. Nowhere was there any hint that the Jewish community cut them off saying that they were no longer Jews. This only happens when Jews choose to follow Yeshua. But faith in him does not cause a person to stop being Jewish, no matter what the Jewish community or the rabbis say. That identity was a sovereign work of Almighty God. No modern rabbi or Jewish leader can change that.

Many rabbis today take the position that a Jew who accepts Yeshua is still a Jew, albeit a wayward Jew. The funeral ceremonies Jewish families once held to mourn a loved one who accepted him do not often take place anymore. This is due, in part, to the strong stand taken nowadays by Jewish believers. We are now more committed to living as Jews, especially our following of the Messiah Yeshua.

In response, the Jewish community senses that Jewish believers in Yeshua are better Jews than they were before. Now they regularly worship the God of Abraham, Isaac, and Jacob. Now they show a stronger commitment to Israel and her survival, based on belief in the Word of God. Many are even moving there.

Ask your Jewish friend if a Jew who practices Buddhism is still Jewish. Ask your Jewish friend if a Jew who is an atheist is still Jewish. Ask your Jewish friend if a Jew who practices yoga is still Jewish. Most likely, the answers will be yes!

Then ask why following a Jew who taught *Torah* and led Jews and Gentiles into a personal relationship with the God of Abraham, Isaac, and Jacob makes one a non-Jew?

To accept Yeshua as Messiah, Savior, and King does not make a Gentile out of a Jew. Yeshua will make your neighbor a Messianic Jew!

"Do you know what will happen in my family if I accept Yeshua as the Messiah and Savior?"

As we just discussed, there was once a time when Jews who accepted Yeshua found themselves unwillingly cut off from their families and friends. It wasn't unusual for the relatives to *sit shiva* (mourn for the dead, as we discussed before) for the wayward son or daughter who professed faith in Yeshua. But, times have changed.

Although it can still be quite upsetting for a family when one among them becomes a believer in Yeshua, it is not as threatening as it once was. In the past, when a Jewish believer joined a church, he often lost his Jewish identity. It no longer was important to marry another Jew, maintain a Jewish lifestyle, and enjoy the culture of the Jewish people.

Since Jews are a minority to begin with, to lose even one is seen as a threat to the very existence of the Jewish people. Therefore, when the life of a new Jewish believer began to revolve around the fellowship of his church, the ignoring of the Jewish community made it seem as if he had left his people. And in many ways, he had.

Nowadays, when a Jew becomes a believer, he can maintain his identity and commitment to his Jewish family, friends, and community. One of the reasons for this has been the growth of the Messianic congregational movement.

Over the past decade, hundreds and hundreds of such congregations have sprung up all over the world. These congregations usually consist of a mixture of Jews and Gentiles who want to worship God in a Jewish way, centered around both the living and written Torah, Yeshua.

The music sounds like other Jewish music. The liturgy contains scripturally appropriate portions from the Jewish prayer books. The holiday celebrations focus on traditional worship enhanced by full Messianic meaning.

For example, *Yom Kippur* is observed with the traditions but always with the recognition that Yeshua has made the final atonement for all sin. Passover is observed acknowledging the full impact of the Messiah, our Passover, as Paul referred to him in 1 Corinthians 5:7, but remembering our deliverance from Egypt.

Many non-Jews enjoy this kind of worship and feel an affinity to the Jewish people and their traditions and customs. There is no "middle wall of partition" in Messianic congregations, as there was in the Temple, separating Jews and Gentiles. Instead Jews and Gentiles worship the one true God together.

Becoming aware of this movement may help you to place your Jewish friend in a worship environment that might help him or her feel at home. "Contextualization" has become a buzzword in mission schools. Missionaries have grown acutely aware of how necessary it is to place the fewest number of stumbling blocks in the path of someone accepting the Good News message. The Messianic congregation is the height of contextualization for Jewish believers.

Understand that if your Jewish friend accepts Yeshua, there might be some negative reaction from family and friends. This is to be expected. But usually after a short time of adjustment, acceptance of his or her new faith will follow. There are people all over the country who can introduce your Jewish neighbor to other Jewish believers who can empathize with what he or she might be experiencing. I'll be sharing how you can connect with a Messianic congregation later.

Happily, there is today a great openness in the Jewish community to the person of Yeshua. Never before in history have so many Jewish scholars considered him a credible Jew. Books are released regularly that discuss Yeshua as a great Jewish leader. We even have a pamphlet called "The Most Famous Jew of All," in which we quote other famous Jews and the nice things they had to say about Yeshua.

This is a great day for sharing the Good News with Jewish people.

"Where was God when the 6,000,000 died?"

This probing question does not relate directly to Yeshua, but rather reflects a relationship, or a non-relationship, with God. For many Jews who lived through the Holocaust, belief in a caring, involved God has become next to impossible. We might have discussed this question under historical barriers to belief. But because of the personal impact the Holocaust had on Jewish people, it fits better in this section.

If God is almighty and cares for his people, how could he let the Nazis kill one-third of his chosen people? As you may expect, this is a very sensitive subject. Frankly, I don't know if anyone has the answer to this dilemma. While it's true that after the Holocaust the nation of Israel was reborn, and that this rebirth was part of God's end-time plan, to throw this out as a justification for the Holocaust is insensitive.

Some say that God promised protection to the Jewish people only when they were living in the land of Israel. Foretold in Scripture were dangers and disasters if the Jews were expelled from the land, something that finally happened in 135 C.E. But again, to point this out to a Jewish person may sound cold and cruel.

One explanation focuses on freedom of choice: "God has given man freedom of choice. He won't step in every time things don't go the way he desires." But does that truth ease the pain of having lost a husband or wife, parent or child, in the Holocaust? No, it doesn't. It's too philosophical. To point this out to a Jewish person may not be sufficient; in fact, it may be insensitive.

I don't think anyone has adequately explained how 6,000,000 of God's chosen people could be allowed to suffer and die as they did.

Better than trying to explain where God was when the 6,000,000 died you might instead try expressing the broken heart of God when any of his people suffer. Our Father in heaven must have suffered like all parents. My father used to tell me that when he had to punish me it hurt him worse than it hurt me. I never believed that. It was my "tush" that was red. I couldn't figure it out. Until I became a father. Now I understand. I must assume that God's suffering exceeded that of his people. He is our heavenly Father.

There's no easy way to break through this barrier to belief. Sympathize with your Jewish neighbor. Empathize if you can. It is possible that he or she lost relatives during that dark day in Jewish history. Your understanding might help undo a little of the hurt that is keeping your friend from faith in God.

You now have a good idea of what personal barriers to belief may keep your Jewish neighbor from faith. These clumps, along with the theological and historical clumps, can really inhibit the birth or growth of the Good News seed planted in Jewish hearts.

But equipped with the right tools and committed to putting in time and patience, you *can* clear the clumps away. You *can* break through the barriers to belief. You *can* overcome Jewish objections to trusting in Yeshua. Prepare yourself as best you can and leave the rest to God. Through your loving witness, Jewish people you know might discover that they are really part of the remnant.

Our last chapter will describe an actual witnessing event. It will serve to summarize much of the material you've already learned and make the point in a fresh way. You've read about this before. It's the story of the woman at the well.

— 16 —

PUTTING IT ALL TOGETHER

— or —

Dropping Your Line For the Lord

It's not enough to understand the "Gentile Great Commission." It's not enough to know how to sensitize your language. It's not even enough to develop a deeper understanding of your Jewish neighbor or co-worker. And finding out how to break down barriers is again only part of the process. We need to put it all together.

At the beginning of this book, I shared the story of my first fishing expedition, to focus on the fact that Yeshua said he'd make his disciples "fishers of men." That was his promise to those who wished to follow him, and although it is 2,000 years later, we, too, are his followers. Now, as always, he wants us to be fishers of men.

Yeshua gave us wonderful instruction in the art of fishing. The Good News of Yochanan (John) recounts the story simply and effectively. It concerns the Messiah and a woman he met at a well. This transaction is a classic example of persuasive communication—an effective witness.

This seems like an appropriate time to summarize a thought that I've tried to weave through this book. If you remember only one thing, I hope it is this: witnessing is nothing more than effectively communicating the Good News of Yeshua, the Messiah—that he came and died to atone for our sins. You might forget much of what I've shared, but if you remember that witnessing to Jewish people is about communicating the truth that the Messiah has come, you've learned a lot.

Yeshua's whole purpose on this earth was to seek and save the lost. Although most of his ministry was directed toward his own people, he surely had a burden for non-Jews. His father sent him to die for their sins too. They too, needed a savior. They needed to receive the gift of eternal life.

The woman at the well was not Jewish. She was a Samaritan, part of a people who developed in the northern kingdom of Israel under Jeroboam after the separation from the southern Kingdom of Judah.

Samaritans were a mixed race with pagan roots, descended from Jews who had intermarried. Keeping many of the same practices of their brethren in Judah, they revered the *Torah*, claiming to have a version even older than that of the Jews. They traced their genealogy back to Jacob. They rejected the rest of the *Tanakh* and developed their own religion, similar to Judaism. The Samaritans were despised by the Jews.

In the fourth chapter of John, Yeshua, a Jew, met a Samaritan woman. Let's now observe Yeshua in this encounter. It's an encouragement to witness. I suggest you read the whole section—John 4:5-30—first, and then let's look at the seven steps in witnessing.

Be Willing

Without question, being willing to witness is the first requirement in any kind of evangelism. Perhaps it seems like an obvious statement, but you have taken that first step by reading a book like this. You have shown your desire to serve the Lord by bringing the Good News to your Jewish neighbor. But you may still need to overcome certain hurdles to continue on your way. Yeshua's example is helpful:

> He came to a town in Shomron [Samaria] called Sh'khem [Sychar], near the field Ya'akov [Jacob] had given his son Yosef [Joseph]. Ya'akov's Well was there; so Yeshua, exhausted from his travel, sat down by the well; it was about noon.
>
> John 4:5-6

Because of his desire to let the Samaritans know that the time had come, he overcame the hurdles that could have stood in the way. He could have offered physical, religious, and social excuses for avoiding the encounter.

In his humanity, Yeshua was tired. He was "exhausted from his travel." We find out later that he was thirsty and hungry. He knew what would happen if he asked this woman to get him a drink—his request would lead to all kinds of questions. It might even have caused him less strain simply to get the drink himself. Yeshua could have thought, "I'm too tired. I need to take care of my physical needs before I can minister to someone else." But he was willing to witness.

A "religious" reason for him to avoid getting involved was that she was a Samaritan. Not only did Jews avoid Samaritans, but observant Jews did not (and still do not) converse publicly with women other than their wives. He could have gotten off the hook and rested. Do we have religious excuses to not associate with some people? Are Jews off limits to you in your mind?

His "social" excuse could have been that this was not the kind of woman with whom he should be seen. Over the course of time, she had had five husbands and the one with whom she was living was not even her husband (John 4:18).

Yeshua could have found a lot of excuses. In his humanity, Yeshua was tired, hungry, and thirsty. He could have come up with a number of physical reasons to not get involved. But Yeshua's willingness to witness overcame these physical obstacles.

Do we get too tired to contact a Jewish friend? Are we too busy? Do we need to take care of our own creature comforts first? Do we find social excuses to not witness? Do we say, "Those people are too _______ (you fill in the blank)"?

Are there any hurdles you need to overcome to witness to your Jewish neighbor? Is your own busy schedule or the potential loss of business a practical physical hurdle? Are there social hurdles such as the discomfort that comes with finding yourself at an event that's culturally different? Are there religious hurdles, such as "they know too much about the Bible"?

Those obstacles can be overcome in the interest of your witness. Begin with prayer. Pray that you will have the boldness to present the Messiah in a clear, forthright way. Pray that your Jewish friend will be willing to listen to you. Pray that the way will be made clear before you, that all the barriers, obstacles, and hurdles might be cleared away, or at least smoothed out a little.

Once you've made up your mind to witness, once you've said you are willing, talk to God about his beloved creature who is your neighbor, your co-worker, or your friend. It is God who placed you in the unique position to witness to the saving gift of the Messiah. Surely, he will help you with your witness . . . if you are willing.

Create Interest

Imagine how surprised the Samaritan woman was when that Jewish man spoke to her! "How is it that you, a Jew, ask for water from me, a woman of Shomron?" (John 4:9) She knew very well that Jews and Samaritans didn't get along, didn't even converse. Her interest was piqued.

This is an example of what social psychologists call cognitive dissonance: two conflicting thoughts, concepts, or ideas being placed together. This well-known principle of social psychology explains many communications.

When I wrote the first edition of this book in 1989, my younger daughter Shira, was creating dissonance. She thought she was playing the piano. Pounding the keys was more like it! The sound was so dissonant it attracted my attention. (Shira gave up piano and is now studying voice; her singing is not dissonant at all; it's beautiful.)

As I write this revised version, my older daughter Rebecca is playing the piano. She takes piano lessons and has become quite accomplished. Rebecca's playing is present in the background, but is not dissonant. I'm enjoying it, but it is not distracting me from writing this.

In music, dissonance is defined as a simultaneous combination of tones in a state of unrest, needing completion. It is an effective tool in music, if used properly. But it can also make for some pretty nasty sounds. One thing is certain, when those dissonant sounds are produced, we notice. Dissonance demands attention!

Yeshua, addressing the woman at the well, caused her to experience cognitive dissonance. Here was a Jewish man speaking to her, a Samaritan woman. That wasn't supposed to happen. A naturally talkative and curious person, the woman immediately became puzzled and challenged Yeshua. Of course, he knew she would.

In your witness to your Jewish friend, you will need to arouse some interest in the Gospel. That's your second step. The way Yeshua did it was to do something out of the ordinary. Dissonance arouses interest. Perhaps you wear a cross. I've already shown how the symbol of the cross can be an affront to Jews. But if your Jewish friend sees you wear a Star of David, that might arouse interest. Asked why you are wearing it, you can respond by saying something like this: "Because Yeshua, the Messiah, was a descendant of King David." Some believers even wear a Star of David with a cross in the middle of it. Talk about arousing interest!

You might ask your Jewish friend if you could attend synagogue sometime with his or her family. Surely that would raise a question or two. If you are asked why, you might say, "Because I'm interested in seeing the kind of service that Yeshua went to. I know he didn't go to church."

There are lines of holiday greeting cards that believers can send to Jewish people to show appreciation and arouse interest. Even adding a personal thought to a standard greeting card for Christian or Jewish holidays can be a way of making that connection. For example, in December, you might send a holiday card to your Jewish friend, saying something like, "I thank God for the Jewish people through whom God brought the Messiah and Savior. Merry Messiahmas!"

You can think of other methods to arouse your neighbor's interest, but let me caution you not to contrive a situation. As I used to explain to my communications classes, someone might arrest attention by firing a rifle before beginning to speak. But unless the message was about hunting or gun control or something gun-related, the rifle shot would be seen as contrived and would ultimately hurt the speaker's credibility.

I urge you to consider pertinent ways to arouse the interest of your Jewish friend. Without first getting your neighbor's attention, no amount of persuasion will succeed.

Be Timely

Whether or not a politician can get legislation passed, balance budgets, or create positive social change, most likely he or she can communicate. This natural ability to persuade, this aptitude for getting elected term after term, comes from having a knack for addressing the concerns of their constituency.

They talk about timely topics, the concerns that matter most. If drug dealers stalk the community, politicians raise their voices in outrage. If pollution is poisoning a river, it will appear on a politician's agenda. The planks of a politician's platform are usually the pertinent affairs of the day. Why? Because timeliness is an essential component of good communication.

Yeshua demonstrated this in his discussion with the woman at the well. She asked him about a Jew talking to a Samaritan and received a timely answer:

> Yeshua answered her, "If you knew God's gift, that is, who it is saying to you, 'Give me a drink of water,' then you would have asked him; and he would have given you living water." She said to him, "Sir, you don't have a bucket, and the well is deep; so where do you get this 'living water'? You aren't greater than our father Ya'akov, are you? He gave us this well and drank from it, and so did his sons and his cattle."
>
> John 4:10–12

His was not the answer the Samaritan woman had anticipated. She had inquired about inter-religious relations—Jews and Samaritans—not water. But in his witness, Yeshua's plan was to get her off of one track and onto another. He planned to move onto spiritual issues in a timely way.

Yeshua had found the woman at the well, not in a store or out in a field. She was there for only one reason—to draw water. What more timely reference could Yeshua have chosen than water? Not only did a timely topic increase her interest, it also led to a spiritual dialogue, as we shall see.

You may recall that in our earlier chapter about discernment we learned that Yeshua sometimes chose not to answer a question directly. In drawing the woman onto the subject of water, and then living water, Yeshua could not have chosen a better way to respond to her question about Jewish-Samaritan relations. In truth, he didn't answer it!

A few years ago, Rabbi Menachem Mendel Schneerson died. His followers believed he was the Messiah and expected him to resurrect soon. My organization got together with another, based in Israel, and published a book called *The Death of Messiah*. It addressed the issue of the Messiahship of Yeshua and what his death, as opposed to Rabbi Schneerson's death, did. It was timely!

How can you be timely with your presentation of the Good News to your Jewish neighbor or friend? To begin with, you can learn through conversation what is on his or her mind. Obviously, the issue of death and resurrection was on the mind of the Lubavitcher Jews who followed Rabbi Schneerson. Your Jewish neighbor has many things on his or her mind. Try to figure out what these might be and see if you can guide your communication toward these things.

Suppose the newspaper reports a major occurrence in Israel. It seems that major events occur there almost daily. As we have said, most American Jews follow news of the Middle East with concern. Why not bring up the news item as an opportunity to discuss what the Bible says about Israel?

Earlier I mentioned a relative of mine with whom I have been sharing. The opportunity arose originally when she expressed to me serious reservations concerning the way world opinion seems to be turning against Israel. I was able to get into the Bible (specifically Zechariah 12 and 14) because of the timeliness of what the Bible has to say about Israel.

Consider what would have happened if I tried to approach her by announcing, "Say, why don't we look into the Bible and study about the Messiah!" Most likely, she would have politely declined.

Israel is generally a timely topic to discuss with your Jewish neighbor. But it is not the only one. The newspaper is full of exciting issues that can lead into Bible discussion. I assure you that if you are willing to witness and seek to arouse interest, you will find many timely topics to discuss.

Speak to Needs

When you attract people's interest and discuss timely topics with them you may well be relating to their needs. By showing how your message can meet these needs, they will be more inclined to hear you out. Yeshua demonstrated this perfectly.

Picture him sitting by Jacob's well. Picture the Samaritan woman approaching him, a water pitcher on each of her shoulders. Feel the hot Israeli sun beating down upon her. It was noon.

After arousing her interest (by simply talking to her) and bringing up a timely topic (water), Yeshua moved the conversation to a deeper level:

> Yeshua answered, "Everyone who drinks this water will get thirsty again, but whoever drinks the water I give him will never be thirsty again! On the contrary, the water I give him will become a spring of water inside him, welling up into eternal life!"

Obviously, Yeshua wasn't talking about H_2O. He was referring to a relationship with God. Jeremiah also used the expression *living water:*

> My people have committed two evils: they have abandoned me, the fountain of living water . . . Jeremiah 2:13

God was the living water. Yeshua was saying that knowing God provided permanent refreshment.

We have all experienced the pleasure of drinking a tall glass of water on a particularly scorching day. There are few things in life that make us feel so good. If we have perspired, if we have become parched, that water offers intense pleasure. Drawing near to God offers a similar satisfaction, but for our spiritual thirst.

Yeshua wanted the Samaritan woman to know God; he wished that she would experience the joy of drinking from the springs of salvation. But he knew he had to lead her to this experience. He could have told her, as he said to others later, "I am the light of the world," but she wasn't looking for a candle. He could have replied, "I am the bread of life," but she wasn't on a picnic. Instead, he spoke about something relevant to her immediate need.

We see that Yeshua was beginning to get onto spiritual subjects. He spoke about "eternal life" (verse 14), but the Samaritan woman did not get his point. Her response was, "Sir, give me this water, so that I won't have to be thirsty and keep coming here to draw water" (verse 15).

She had no idea what Yeshua was talking about, and yet somehow she wanted what he was offering. Tired of traipsing back and forth to this well every day in the hot Israeli sun to get a few pitchers of water, she had a real need. Although Yeshua was interested in her deeper need, he decided to address her in the context of her present need.

We, as his students, ought to model ourselves after our rabbi. If we seek the kind of spirituality evidenced by Yeshua, if we look for ways to be like him, let us share with people as he did—with relevance, observing people's circumstances for the context of our communications, in other words, dealing with people's needs.

It might sound manipulative, but it's not. It's effective. A good communicator always attempts to understand the needs of those to whom he is communicating. Communication ethics require that interest be sincere. Surely the one who gave his life for the sin of the world is our greatest example of sincere interest in others.

If a man you knew was about to drive off a cliff, naturally you'd try to warn him. Well, unless your Jewish friends have eternal life, they are headed toward that cliff. It is imperative that your witness speak to their needs.

In *Motivation and Personality*, the famous humanistic psychologist Abraham Maslow described what he called a hierarchy of people's needs. He reduced mankind's needs into five basic categories; physiology, safety, belongingness, esteem, and self-actualization. Maslow concluded that each level of need must be satisfied before a person can move on to the next level.

Maslow would probably not define his message in scriptural terms; still, I like his structure because it seems to move, in biblical language, from the flesh to the spirit. A good communicator must know the level on which he must speak in order to deliver his message successfully. A missionary to the down-and-out is not going to begin ministering by bringing up the subject of eternal life. If the person he's talking to is starving, the worker must first see to it that he is fed. That, of course, is the approach taken by many inner-city rescue missions.

But, as a general rule, especially in America, there are not many hungry Jews. Except for a minority of older people or Russian immigrants who live in pockets of poverty, Jewish people today can be found in the middle class or better. So if the person you want to witness to is physiologically satisfied—fed, rested, warm—then you must discover the level of his greatest need.

Perhaps he does not feel safe or secure. Perhaps he doesn't feel loved. Maybe circumstances have denied him self-esteem. According to Maslow, all these must be addressed before the person can become self-actualized. A self-actualized person is one who is living at his own maximum potential. This person is more altruistic. He might be concerned with spiritual things. Until a person's first four needs are satisfied, it is less likely that he or she will seek to satisfy this higher need.

When we witness, we do well to understand the needs of those with whom we share. Although Jewish people are not generally hungry or ill-housed, there are many who feel a need for safety or security, particularly because of rising anti-Semitism and anti-Israel attitudes.

Also, you'll often find a need for belongingness. Your offer of friendship and fellowship as well as your commitment to the Jewish people and the land of Israel may speak to some of those safety and belongingness needs. In other words, be a real friend.

Establish Expertness

We spoke earlier about credibility, that extra something that makes one person more believable than another. You can develop a more credible testimony with every encounter. The way you relate to your family says something about how your faith operates. Your business dealings reveal further the reliability of that faith. Your works testify to the worth of your belief. Each of these adds to—or detracts from—your credibility quotient.

In John 4:16–19, Yeshua uses his supernatural powers to establish supernatural credibility. He was an expert! We, too, can exhibit expertness when witnessing to our Jewish friends. Remember, up until this point Yeshua was just a tired, hungry, thirsty Jew who was violating Jewish tradition!

> He said to her, "Go, call your husband, and come back." She answered, "I don't have a husband." Yeshua said to her, "You're right, you don't have a husband! You've had five husbands in the past, and you're not married to the man you're living with now! You've spoken the truth!"

He knew her heart. He knew her darkest secrets. He knew she was a sinner, yet he did not condemn her. Somehow, this Jew she had never met before knew everything about her. He was an expert in knowing her. "How amazing!" she must have thought. Perhaps she could ask him some religious questions. And this is exactly what she did.

Jewish people, like all people, yearn to know about the spiritual world. They watch television shows, videos, and movies about the occult, mysticism, and the supernatural.

But it's the rare rabbi who teaches about angels, demons, heaven, hell, the Messiah, or resurrection. This is not the content of your average Sabbath morning sermon. Oh, sure, there are readings from the *Tanakh* and often the readings serve as a jumping-off point for the sermon. But, too often, what is missing is a sense of reality concerning Bible events. Somehow, I'm sad to say, many of my people have lost their sense of the supernatural, relegating God to the status of a rabbinical tradition.

Often the miracles of the Bible are described as mere natural events that a superstitious and backward people attributed to what they called "God." It would not be surprising to hear discussion of "the myths of the Bible." The sense of awe has vanished from the worship of the majority of Jewish people.

For the most part, then, Jews would not go to their rabbis to discuss issues of the supernatural. But, oddly enough, they might come to you if they are convinced that you truly believe in the supernatural. You may have the opportunity to explain things to your Jewish neighbor that he or she might not find answers to anywhere else—information concerning the Bible or God or the afterlife.

As I shared before, when I met the Rigneys, who introduced me to the Messiah, I was very thirsty to talk about spiritual things. One rabbi I spoke to was controlled by the *Talmud* and wouldn't discuss certain "forbidden" subjects. The other rabbi didn't even believe in God. My spiritual thirst demanded answers. The Rigneys were trustworthy and knowledgeable about the Bible as well as about the Jewish people; I had plenty to ask them. They had the answers to my questions.

Your Jewish friend may be thirsting for information about spiritual things. He or she may have wrestled with questions for decades. If you display evidence of credibility, your neighbor might ask *you*.

Open Up the Scriptures

The woman at the well sensed Yeshua's credibility. He knew all about her and still he talked to her. He accepted her, a major-league sinner. He was trustworthy and expert, two of the four factors that make a person credible. Here was an opportunity to ask questions that may have been bothering her for years:

> Our fathers worshipped on this mountain [Gerizim], but you people say that the place where men ought to worship is in Yerushalayim [Jerusalem]. John 4:20

Even though it sounded like a statement, this lady was asking a question. Yeshua heard it, and answered her:

> Yeshua said, "Lady, believe me, the time is coming when you will worship the Father neither on this mountain nor in Yerushalayim. You people don't know what you are worshipping; we worship what we do know, because salvation comes from the Jews. . . . God is spirit; and worshippers must worship him spiritually and truly." John 4:21-22, 24

Recognizing Yeshua's credibility, she asked the question about worship—Gerizim or Jerusalem? Yeshua used this opportunity to discuss scriptural subjects. She asked about the place of worship; he answered about salvation.

The hour of salvation was upon her, he explained. Salvation was to come through the Jews. Furthermore, God had a way he wanted people to worship him that did not merely involve location—God wanted to be worshipped properly.

Keep in mind that it took only a few minutes for this woman to feel comfortable and trusting enough to talk about these controversial issues. Yeshua was drawing her into the truth. Once he got to the spiritual subjects of salvation and worship, the "close" was not far away.

Introduce Salvation

Suppose that when this lady with her pitcher of water had approached the well, Yeshua had stood up and said, "Hi, I'm the Messiah. Got a drink?" In modern-day vernacular she might have responded, "Sure, buddy, and I'm the Queen of England." He was tired, hungry, sweaty, and dressed in the clothes of a working man, not the royal robes of a king. Not exactly Messiah-looking! The woman might well have walked away from this "nut." But she didn't do this. His approach was slowly revealing; he moved carefully, following through, step by step, until *she* asked *him* if *he* might indeed be the Messiah.

> The woman replied, "I know that *Mashiach* [Messiah] is coming. When he comes he will tell us everything." Yeshua said to her, "I, the person speaking to you, am he."
>
> John 4:25-26

I can't help thinking that she had some hint that he was the Messiah. I hear a question mark at the end of her statement. She was ready. It was time. She believed. She left her water pot and broadcast the news all over town. "Come, see a man who told me everything I've ever done. Could it be that this is the Messiah?" How many people believed as a result of hearing her testimony is hard to say. But surely many did. Yeshua caught a lot of fish that day. There's no reason you can't as well.

Yeshua was *willing* to witness, even though he had plenty of excuses to take it easy. He got her *interest* by just speaking to her. He was *timely* in his use of the "living water" image. He spoke to her *need*, even though she misinterpreted it. He demonstrated his *expertise* by knowing what she was really like inside. He got into a *scriptural* discussion when she was ready. Finally, he introduced himself as the *Savior* when she asked.

I've created an acronym to help you remember these principles: **W.I.T.N.E.S.S.**

Willingness
Interest
Timeliness
Need
Expertness
Scripture
Salvation

The master fisherman promised that he would make his disciples fishers of men. May these seven steps help you as you fish—for sheep— for the lost sheep of the house of Israel.

If I or my organization can offer any help to you as you set about to share the Messiah—help obtaining Messianic Jewish resources, help locating your nearest Messianic congregation, or help answering questions you may have—contact me at Lederer/Messianic Jewish Communications, P.O. Box 615, Clarksville, MD 21029. Our e-mail address is Lederer@messianicjewish.net; our website www.MessianicJewish.net.

God bless you as you fulfill your Great Commission—and good fishing!

EPILOGUE

A few last words of personal testimony . . .

It was April 16, 1973, the day after *Tax Return Day*. I was working for my father's C.P.A. firm. He took the whole office sailing as reward for a successful tax season. It took place while we were sailing on the Chesapeake Bay.

We were moving along beneath the Bay Bridge. I looked up to watch some of the construction, marveling at the new span being added to the old bridge. Suddenly the serenity was shattered as a piece of steel tumbled from the bridge, crashing down onto our boat. It landed with an ear-splitting crack, so close to me that it broke my watch crystal. Fortunately, it did not break through the bottom of the boat.

The others I was with raced over to where I stood, their voices high-pitched, full of panic and disbelief. Yet only one thought reached through to my numbed consciousness: Would God bring about something like this to make his point? Scripture *does* teach that Jews seek for a sign. But this? Or was *HaSatan*, the Adversary, trying to kill me before I received salvation in the Messiah?

I found that I was strangely calm about the fact that I had almost been crushed by the piece of falling steel. What made me shake, though, was the enormity of the spiritual decision that lay before me. Although I had studied Isaiah 53, although I had calculated the time of the coming of Messiah from Daniel 9, although I had understood a Jew could believe in Yeshua, I was still reluctant to yield my life to the Messiah. I had spent half of a year mulling it over.

That night I attended a Passover Seder, the service that recounts the freeing of the Jewish people from slavery in Egypt thousands of years ago. It was a Messianic service led by Dan Rigney. The commemorative dinner was held in Baltimore at a place called The Lederer Foundation, the organization I now serve as president. I listened as the elements of Passover were described with their full Messianic meaning. I asked questions of Dr. Henry Einspruch, a distinguished *Torah* and *Talmud* scholar, head of The Lederer Foundation. I knew I now believed.

That night, in the quietness of my home, I told the God of Abraham, Isaac, and Jacob that I believed Yeshua was the Messiah, sent to be my Savior. I fell asleep peacefully for the first time in six months. Like Jonah, who ultimately yielded to the Lord, I too knew I could run no longer.

It was later that I discovered how many people had been praying for me in Baltimore, Washington, and all across the country! From time to time I still meet people who were praying for me back in 1972. One of those people who was praying was a nice Jewish girl, originally from the Bronx, named Steffi. She and I met a few months after I received Yeshua. We were married two years later and God has since blessed us with two lovely daughters.

You want your Jewish friend to meet the Messiah. So does God. Start to pray; ask others to do the same. This is spiritual warfare and God has called you to do battle. Your most powerful weapon is heartfelt prayer.

Have your Jewish neighbor bring the bagels. You bring the Gospel. Soon we'll hear the angels in heaven rejoicing over the salvation of some of the remnant of God's chosen people. You can do it.

Glossary of Jewish Terms

These are common Hebrew and Yiddish words used by Jewish people. Hebrew, of course, is the ancient language of the Jewish people and the official language of the State of Israel. Yiddish is a language spoken by Eastern European Jews that uses Hebrew letters and sounds like German. It is spoken by many European and American Jews. If you understand these words, it will help you communicate better with Jewish people.

Adonai	"Lord"; Since the Hebrew name of "God", YHWH, is not used by Jews because it is too holy to pronounce, *Adonai* is a substitute. *HaShem*, "The Name," is also used.
Aliyah	"going up"; immigrating to *Eretz Yisra'el*, the Land of Israel. Also, when a person "goes up" to read from the *Torah*, he makes an *aliyah*.
Ashkenazi	a Jew from Eastern, Central or Western European origin (Poland, Russia, Germany, France, etc.)
Bar Mitzvah	"Son of the Commandment"; a boy who has reached age 13, the age of religious maturity, and who has a ceremony accepting responsibility for his ways before God
Bat Mitzvah	"Daughter of the Commandment"; a girl who has reached the age of religious maturity

	between 12 and 13 and who has a ceremony accepting responsibility for her ways before God
Bimah	during a synagogue service, the place from where the Torah is read and sermons are given
B'nai B'rith	"sons of the covenant"; a Jewish fraternal organization founded in 1843
B'rakhah	"blessing"; offered on any occasion that calls for praise
B'ris; B'rit Milah	"covenant of circumcision"; occurs when a boy is 8 days old (see Genesis 17:9–14)
Chag Sameyach	"happy holiday"; a greeting
Chasid	"pious one"; follower of *Chasidism*, an ultra-Orthodox sect
Chazzan	"cantor"; usually the leader of the liturgical part of the service
Chupah	the bridal canopy denoting God's presence in the new home and a reminder of the Temple at Jerusalem, symbolic of God's dwelling place with man
Eretz Yisra'el	"Land of Israel"
Goy	"Gentile"; pl. *goyim*, nations
Gut Yom Tov	"good holiday"; Yiddish word
Haftarah	the section of the Prophets read immediately after the reading of the *Torah* at *Shabbat* services and on most holidays
Haggadah	"the telling"; the Passover story; also the ritual manual used for the *Pesach* service
Halakhah	"the way"; tradition, practice, rule in Judaism
Hallel	"praise"; root word of *halleluyah*; refers to certain psalms of praise
Hanukkah	"dedication"; celebrates the rededication of the Temple of the Lord by the Maccabees in 165 B.C.E. Also known as the Festival of Lights
Hatikvah	"The Hope"; Israel's national anthem
Kabbalah	Jewish mysticism

Kaddish	"holy"; praise to God recited in memorial to the departed
Kashrut	the dietary laws
Kiddush	"sanctify"; the benediction over the "fruit of the vine" (wine) to sanctify (make holy or set apart) *Shabbat* and holidays
Kol Nidrey	"All Vows"; chanted on the eve of *Yom Kippur*
Kosher	clean, acceptable food in accordance with Jewish law, especially excluding pork and shellfish (Deuteronomy 14:3–21)
L'chayyim	"to life!"; a toast or salute
K'tuvah	Jewish marriage contract
K'tuvim	"Writings"; includes historical and poetical books of the Bible
L'hitra'ot	"until we meet again"; goodbye
L'Shanah Tovah	"to a good year!"; a New Year's greeting
Magen David	"shield of David"; a six pointed star commonly worn by Jews and used as a symbol of the Jewish people
Mashiach	"Anointed One"; Messiah
Matzah	"unleavened bread"; used exclusively during Passover and the Feast of Unleavened Bread
Mazel Tov	"good luck"; congratulations
Menorah	"candelabra"; seven-branched (Exodus 25:31–37) except during *Hanukkah*, when a nine-branched menorah is used.
M'gillot	"scrolls"; part of the *K'tuvim*, including the books of Esther (known as The M'gillah), Lamentations, Song of Solomon, Ruth, and Ecclesiastes
Mikveh	"the ritual bath for purification"; forerunner of the Christian "baptism."
Minyan	"quorum" needed for a service; ten men thirteen years or older
Mitzvah	"commandment"; in common usage, a good deed
M'shummad	"an apostate Jew"; one who "converts" to "Christianity"

M'zuzah "doorpost"; a parchment scroll usually in a metal container attached to the doorpost on the right side of the entrance to a house or room (Deuteronomy 6:9); contains the *Sh'ma* (Deuteronomy 6:4-11) and other Scripture (Deuteronomy 11:13-21); also worn as jewelry

Ner Tamid "eternal light"; a perpetual light in the synagogue signifying God's presence

Nevi'im "Prophets"; the books of the prophets

Pesach "Passover"; in practice, synonymous with the Feast of Unleavened Bread (Exodus 12:14-20; Leviticus 23:5-8)

Purim "lots"; also the Feast of Esther, celebrating the victory over Haman and those who sought Jewish extinction. Based on the book of Esther.

Rosh HaShanah "Head of the Year"; the Jewish New Year, celebrated usually in September or October; actually the Feast of Trumpets (Leviticus 23:24-25)

Ruach HaKodesh "Holy Spirit"

Seder "order"; the Passover service (and dinner) usually conducted on the first and second nights of Passover

S'fardi a Jewish person from Eastern, Oriental, or Southern Mediterranean origins (Turkey, Spain, Egypt, etc.)

Shabbat "Sabbath"; Friday sunset to Saturday sunset (Leviticus 23:3)

Shalom "peace"; used instead of "hello" or "goodbye"

Shalom Aleykhem "peace be unto you"

Shammash "servant"; the caretaker or sexton of the synagogue or temple; also the ninth candle on the *Chanukkah* menorah

Shavu'ot "Weeks"; The Feast of Weeks or Pentecost (Leviticus 23:15-21)

Shiva "seven"; the seven-day mourning period after the death of a loved one

Sh'ma	"Hear"; Jewish affirmation of faith (Deuteronomy 6:4) recited morning and evening by religious Jews and during all worship services
Shul	"school"; another word for an Orthodox or *Chasidic* synagogue for the study of the *Torah*
Shulchan Arukh	the codified laws of rabbinical Judaism
Siddur	"prayer book"; contains prayers, Scripture, and order of service
Simchat Torah	"Rejoicing of the Law"; conclusion of the public synagogue reading cycle of the *Torah* each year
Sukkah	"booth"; used during *Sukkot* for meals and/or sleeping
Sukkot	"booths"; Feast of Tabernacles (Leviticus 23:33–36)
Synagogue	"assembly"; usually Orthodox or Conservative Jewish house of worship
Tallit	"prayer shawl"; worn during worship in the synagogue or at home
Talmud	"study"; the oral traditions, discussions, and instructions in 37 volumes (Hebrew/English) of the great rabbis of Judaism (100 B.C.E. to 200 C.E.). Commentary on the *Tanakh*, "the written law"
Talmud Torah	a community religious school teaching Hebrew, *Talmud*, *Torah*, and secular subjects as well
Tanakh	"*Torah*, *N'vi'im*, *K'tuvim* (T-N-K)"; the Old Testament
Temple	Reform Jewish house of worship
T'fillin	"phylacteries"; leather boxes attached to leather thongs wound around the head and arm, used by very religious Jews during prayer. The box contains portions of the *Torah* (Deuteronomy 6:8)
Torah	"Law"; the five books of Moses, also known as the *Chumash*

Treyfe "unacceptable food"; also, not in accordance with God's ways; a Yiddish word

Tzaddik "righteous one"; usually applied to a spiritual leader, one who is learned and pious

Tzitzit "fringes" attached to the four corners of the *tallit* (Numbers 15:38–40)

Yahrzeit the anniversary of the death of a loved one; a Yiddish word

Yarmulke "skullcap"; a Yiddish word; used to cover mens' heads, especially during worship in the synagogue or home (also called *kippah* or "covering")

Yizkor "may he remember"; the memorial to the dead

Yom HaBikkurim "Day of First fruits"; associated with resurrection (Leviticus 23:10–14)

Yom Kippur "Day of Atonement"; holiest day of the Jewish year, observed with fasting and prayers for forgiveness (Leviticus 23:26–32)

Y'shivah a religious school of higher learning

Zion "Israel"

Zionist one who supports the idea of a Jewish state, namely, Israel

Selected Bibliography

Ausubel, Nathan, ed. *A Treasury of Jewish Humor*. Garden City, N.J.: Doubleday and Company, Inc., 1951.

Goldberg, M. Hirsch. *The Jewish Connection*. New York: Stein and Day, 1976.

Grayzel, Solomon. *A History of the Jews*. Philadelphia: Jewish Publication Society, 1970.

Kjær-Hansen, Kai, ed., *The Death of Messiah*. Baltimore: Lederer Publishers, 1994.

Lapide, Pinchas. *The Resurrection of Jesus*. Minneapolis: Augsburg Publishing House, 1983.

Maslow, Abraham. *Motivation and Personality*. New York: Harper and Row, 1954.

Phillips, McCandlish. *The Bible, The Supernatural, and the Jews.* Minneapolis: Bethany Fellowship, 1970. (Available from Messianic Jewish Resources Intl., 800-410-7367.)

Potok, Chaim. *The Chosen*. New York: Fawcett Crest, 1967.

——. *My Name is Asher Lev*. Greenwich, Conn.: Fawcett Crest,

1972.

Rosten, Leo. *The Joys of Yiddish*. New York: McGraw-Hill Book Company, 1968.

Stern, David. *Complete Jewish Bible*. Clarksville, Md.: Jewish New Testament Publications, Inc., 1998.

Ten Boom, Corrie. *The Hiding Place*. Grand Rapids, Mich.: Chosen Books, 1984.

Suggested Reading

Available Through
Messianic Jewish Resources International

Kasdan, Barney. *God's Appointed Times*. Clarksville, MD: Messianic Publishers, 1993.

——. *God's Appointed Customs*. Clarksville, MD: Messianic Publishers, 1996.

Moseley, Ron. *Yeshua: A Guide to the Real Jesus and the Original Church*. Clarksville, MD: Messianic Jewish Publishers, 1998.

Rudolph, David, ed. *The Voice of the Lord*. Clarksville, MD: Messianic Jewish Publishers, 1998.

Stern, David H., trans. *Jewish New Testament Commentary*. Clarksville, MD: Jewish New Testament Publications, Inc., 1989.

——. *Restoring the Jewishness of the Gospel*. Clarksville, MD: Jewish New Testament Publications, Inc., 1990.

Study and Discussion Questions

If you write out the answers to these questions and send them to our office, addressed to "Bagels Course," we will send you a beautiful, color certificate of completion that affirms you as a "lover of Israel."

You will be able to display this so Jewish people might look at it and ask you about it. We ask that you include a check for $10 to cover the cost of the certificate, shipping and handling.

Chapter One

1. What are the four special reasons to share the Messiah with Jewish people?
2. What is the Biblical concept of the remnant?
3. What does Genesis 12:3 say and why is it important in Jewish outreach?
4. What is the greatest blessing you can bring to a Jewish person?

Chapter Two

1. What is the Gentile's role in Jewish evangelism?
2. Describe the "proper attitude" toward unbelieving Jewish people.

Chapter Three

1. Explain the Jewish revolt of 134 C.E.
2. Many of the early church leaders instituted new traditions and laws governing the relationship between Christians and Jews. Briefly describe them.
3. What impact did the Crusades have on Jewish people?
4. How would you explain to a Jewish person the difference between Christianity and Nazism?

Chapter Four

1. Define credibility.
2. How can you become more trustworthy to your Jewish neighbor?
3. Can you be an "expert" in the Bible when talking with a Jewish person? How?
4. What are some ways you can identify with Jewish people?
5. What are the three foundation blocks upon which credibility is built?

Chapter Five

1. Define *Tanakh*.
2. List and describe three premises that you can relate to your Jewish neighbor.

Chapter Six

1. Name some useful Messianic prophecies, briefly describe them, and quote the Scripture references.
2. What was the rabbinic interpretation of Isaiah 53 before Rashi?
3. What is the present Jewish view of Isaiah 53?
4. Explain the two-Messiah theory.

Chapter Seven

The following is a list of commonly used Christian terms that may be offensive to a Jewish person. Give the "Messianic" alternative:

Christian (as an adjective) ________________________
Christian (as a noun) ________________________
Christ ________________________
Church ________________________
Jesus ________________________
Died for my sins ________________________
Holy Spirit/Holy Ghost ________________________
Trinity ________________________
Gospel ________________________
Easter ________________________
Christmas ________________________
Pentecost ________________________
Second coming of Christ ________________________
New Testament ________________________
Old Testament ________________________
Baptism ________________________
Cross ________________________
Conversion ________________________

Chapter Eight

1. Name some physical stereotypes that Christians may have of Jewish people.
2. List some spiritual stereotypes about Jewish people.
3. In what ways do Jewish people share the same theology? In what ways are there differences?

Chapter Nine

1. Who was the first Jew?
2. Describe the development of the rabbinic office.
3. Who was Judah Maccabee?
4. John 10:22 describes Yeshua partaking in a celebration. What was the celebration?
5. Describe some events that caused the assimilation of Jewish believers into the early Church.
6. What was the first official Jewish settlement in America?
7. What happened on November 9-10, 1938?
8. Describe the Balfour Declaration.
9. Give the date that Israel became a nation in modern history.

Chapter Ten

1. By 100 B.C.E. there were three main religious sects in Judaism. Name them.
2. The *Talmud* is also called what?
3. What are the two bodies of work that comprise the *Talmud*?
4. There are four main branches of modern Judaism. Name and briefly describe each.

Chapter Eleven

1. Name the two major origins of the modern Jewish people.
2. What is a *Shtetl*?
3. Describe a *Bar Mitzvah*.
4. Define *Kashrut*.
5. Name some foods that are not *kosher*.
6. What is meant by putting a "fence around the Law?"
7. Jewish people have a unique ceremony for the birth of a baby boy. Name and describe this ceremony.

8. What is a *chupah*?
9. Explain the expression "sitting *shiva*."

Chapter Twelve

1. What is a "challenging question?" How would you handle it?
2. What is a "trap question?" How would you handle it?
3. What is a "false question?" How would you handle it?
4. What is a "testing question?" How would you handle it?

Chapter Thirteen

1. Name some historical barriers to belief in Yeshua.
2. What is your answer to the accusation that "the New Testament is anti-Semitic?"
3. Do rabbis believe that Yeshua is the Messiah?
4. Do Jews proselytize? Have they ever?

Chapter Fourteen

1. Explain the difference between the two Hebrew words *echad* and *yachid*.
2. What is the Sonship of Yeshua?
3. Does the Bible teach substitutionary atonement? What does this term mean?
4. Why is there no peace on earth today?

Chapter Fifteen

1. What does the Bible teach about "good people?"
2. When a Jewish person comes to believe in Yeshua, does he or she lose his or her Jewishness? Explain.

3. How would you help a Jewish person who is afraid to accept Yeshua because he or she feels they will lose his or her friends or family?
4. In trying to answer, "Where was God when the 6,000,000 died," what is the best approach?

Chapter Sixteen

1. In the chapter "Putting it all together," you learned the acronym WITNESS. Explain this acronym.
2. What do you feel you have learned from studying this book?

ABOUT THE AUTHOR

BARRY RUBIN was born in New York City in 1945, the year his family moved to Washington, D.C., ultimately settling in Maryland. After graduating high school, he went to Ohio University in Athens, Ohio and obtained a bachelor's degree in Organizational Communications and a master's degree in Interpersonal Communications.

In 1973, after a spiritual search, he became convinced that Yeshua—Jesus—of Nazareth was the Messiah and began following his teachings.

From 1974 to 1988 he worked with several organizations that proclaimed the message that the Messiah has come. In 1981 he became the rabbi of Emmanuel Messianic Jewish Congregation, the oldest extant Messianic congregation in the country (c. 1915). He still serves this congregation, which now meets in Howard County, Maryland.

In 1988, he became president and C.E.O. of The Lederer Foundation (now, Messianic Jewish Communications). In 1989, he became executive vice president and C.E.O. of Jewish New Testament Publications, Inc.

He has served on the editorial board of the International Messianic Jewish Alliance, and was the publisher of *Messianic Jewish*

Life, its magazine. He has also served on the board of St. Petersburg Theological Seminary.

Mr. Rubin was listed in *Who's Who in the East, Who's Who in Religion*, and *Who's Who Among Professionals*. He enjoys golf and crossword puzzles. His wife, Steffi, also a Jewish believer in Yeshua, illustrated this book, and is an accomplished graphic artist and songwriter. Both their children, Rebecca and Shira, have been active in their congregation.

ABOUT MESSIANIC JEWISH COMMUNICATIONS

Messianic Jewish Communications was incorporated as The Lederer Foundation in 1949, although it had been in operation for decades before under other names. Dr. Henry Einspruch and his wife, Marie, started the work to help inquiring Jewish people meet the Messiah. They published the *Yiddish New Testament* and other books useful in evangelism and education. Lewis and Harriet Lederer contributed funds to make possible the printing of the *Yiddish New Testament*, thus the name.

The organization has expanded over the years. The new name Messianic Jewish Communications reflects this expansion. The publishing division is called Messianic Jewish Publishers. Other divisions include Messianic Jewish Resources International, which markets and distributes Messianic books, music and teaching cassettes and CDs, Judaica and gifts from Israel; Messianic Jewish Ministries, the outreach arm; and Messianic Jewish Church Programs, the teaching arm.

The administrative office of Messianic Jewish Communications can be reached by emailing us at lederer@messianicjewish.net, or writing 6120 Day Long Lane, Clarksville, MD 21029.

All of the products distributed by Messianic Jewish Resources International can be purchased through our online catalog at: http://www.MessianicJewish.net or by calling (800) 410-7367.